London International Conferences

PROCEEDINGS 2021-1

January 2021

London International Conferences, 28-30 January 2021, hosted online by UKEY Consulting and Publishing, London, United Kingdom

UKEY

CONSULTING & PUBLISHING

LONDONIC.UK

ISBN: 9798723428867

Proceeding: London International Conference, January 2021

Presenters:	**Durairaj Rajan**
	Olga Nosova
	Joy Onyinyechi Ekwoaba
	Christopher Odogwu Chidi
	Konstantin P. Taushanzhi
	S. I. Anastasov
	R. Malini
	E. Shanmugapriya
	Abubakar Tanko Mohammed
	Selim Ozdemir
	Mehmet Ali Eroğlu
	Teymur Valiyev
	R. Raghadevi
	R. A. Aruna
	Serife Metin
	Yakup Doğanay
	İbrahim Kurt
	Mehmet Tas
	Vahap Odar
Editor:	**Omar Farooq**
Design:	Studio Ima
Cover:	**Itaco**
Publisher:	**UKEY Publishing**
Version:	**V01**
Series:	**Proceedings 01**

Copyright © 2021 UKEY Publishing

ukeyconsultingpublishing.co.uk

ISBN: 9798723428867

Contents

londonic.uk   ukeyconsultingpublishing.co.uk

Role and Compensation Related Factors Causing Heavy Workload: An Empirical Study among Sanitary Workers

Durairaj Rajan
Department of Business Administration
Faculty of Social and Management Sciences
University of Africa, Toru-Orua (UAT), Bayelsa State, Nigeria
drdirajan@gmail.com

Abstract

This survey, quantitative and empirical based descriptive research has the objective of analysing perception of sanitary workers working in private multi-speciality hospitals in Tirunelveli city of Tamil Nadu, India towards various role and compensation related factors causing heavy workload. In order to achieve the objective, the study sampled 80 respondents using both convenience and judgement sampling techniques, and from the chosen respondents the primary data were collected using schedule method with the help of questionnaire (translating the questions in respondents' mother language, 'Tamil') along with interview. The secondary data were collected from books, journals and conference proceedings to add appropriate significance to the study. Percentage method was administered to analyse both demographic characteristics of the study and perception of the respondents towards role and compensation related factors causing heavy workload. The result of the analysis has found that all the factors discussed in

London International Conferences, 28-30 January 2021, hosted online by UKEY Consulting and Publishing, London, United Kingdom

this study such as ill-defined roles and responsibilities, receiving conflicting messages from two or more heads at the same time, person's interest remain contradict with the job role, salary is not adequate in accordance with the work performed, discrimination and bias in fixing salary and inadequate non-monetary rewards for effective contribution at work were strongly agreed by majority of the respondents. The study has given suitable suggestions as to how to rationalize the role and compensation related factors causing heavy workload.

Keywords: Role, compensation, workload, sanitary worker, private hospital, Tirunelveli city

London International Conferences

londonic.uk   ukeyconsultingpublishing.co.uk

System Transformational Changes in Ukraine

Olga Nosova
V.N. Karasin Kharkiv National University
olgano59@gmail.com

Abstract

The article aims to study and analyzes the political and social-economic changes in the process of system transformation in Ukraine from 1991 to 2018. The paper represents an attempt to understand the content of system transformation, causes of successful and inefficient practices, and proposes recommendations for its improvement.

The hypothesis of the study is to estimate how the GDP in Ukraine depends on the degree of economic, political, social transformation, as well as the overall indicators (market and democratic) transformation. The study discusses the concepts of system transformation, describe types of transformation, determine the impact of transformational changes on economic growth in a country, analyses GDP relationship from transformational changes, contributing, and slowing down factors.

Keywords: system transformation, transformational change, economic growth.

London International Conferences, 28-30 January 2021, hosted online by UKEY Consulting and Publishing, London, United Kingdom

London International Conferences

londonic.uk   ukeyconsultingpublishing.co.uk

Wages and Salaries Determination and Adjustments in the Nigerian Public Sector

Joy Onyinyechi Ekwoaba
Department of Employment Relations & Human Resource Management,
Faculty of Management Sciences, University of Lagos
ekwoaba2002@yahoo.com

Christopher Odogwu Chidi
Department of Employment Relations & Human Resource Management
Faculty of Management Sciences, University of Lagos
ochidi@unilag.edu.ng

Abstract

The authors reviewed wages and salaries determination and adjustments in the Nigerian public sector from 1934 to 2014. The authors observed that the use of ad-hoc wage commissions in the determination of wages and a host of other conditions of service has hampered effective collective bargaining in the Nigerian public sector. Other issues discussed are the Labour Act, Employees' Compensation Act, the Minimum Wage Act, Pension Scheme, and the National Health Insurance Scheme.

The authors adopted the qualitative research approach and relied on secondary source of data based on the review of literature.

London International Conferences, 28-30 January 2021, hosted online by UKEY Consulting and Publishing, London, United Kingdom

Workers' pay or compensation is regulated through government labour policy as stipulated by the Nigerian labour laws or legislation. These laws include the Labour Act, the Employees' Compensation Act, the Minimum Wage Act, the Pension Act, and the National Health Insurance Act. The provisions of these labour policies have both positive and negative implications for the Nigerian workers. It is hereby recommended that the adoption of collective bargaining and the commitment on the part of the government to abide by the ensuing agreement with unions in the public sector is the surest means for promoting peaceful labour-government relations and to a large extent forestall incessant strikes that have bedevilled the public sector in recent times. There is the need for the Ministry of Labour and Employment to be alive to its responsibilities by ensuring that government labour policies and laws are implemented to the letter. There is the urgent need to step up labour administration and inspection by the Ministry. With regard to the embezzlement of pension funds, there should be stiff penalties imposed on those who mismanage or embezzle such funds and the penalty should be life imprisonment or capital punishment. On the issue of health for employees and Nigerians in general, there is a need to expand the NHIS to accommodate workers in the informal sector and those in the rural areas for the impact to be more felt and visible. Robust budgetary allocations should be allotted to the health sector every year to meet the health needs of workers and Nigerians. In the same vein, the state-of-the-art-medical facilities and centres should be established in the six geo-political zones to meet the health needs of the teeming Nigerians and to reduce medical tourism abroad. This of course will assist to conserve foreign exchange which can be ploughed back to the economy for developmental projects that will benefit the citizenry.

London International Conferences, 28-30 January 2021, hosted online by UKEY Consulting and Publishing, London, United Kingdom

Employee compensation is critical in any employment relationship and a major source of conflict in labour-management relations.

Keywords: Wages and Salaries Determination, Adjustments, Public Sector, Nigeria

London International Conferences, 28-30 January 2021, hosted online by UKEY Consulting and Publishing, London, United Kingdom

1. Introduction

The Nigerian government is the single largest employer of labour as elsewhere in the globe/world. Employee compensation is critical in employment relationship and a major source of conflict in labour-management relations. The involvement of the Nigerian government in workers' compensation (wages and salaries) began at the turn of the 19th century arising from the emergence of wage labour (Fashoyin, 1992). A wage is used specifically to refer to payment to hourly-rated production and service workers and represents direct monetary compensation; whereas, salary is generally paid to administrative, professional and managerial employees. Salaries are calculated on a monthly or annual basis (Yoder & Staudohar, 1982). There are three broad methods by which wages, salaries and conditions of service are determined in Nigeria. These are the individual-employer contract, collective bargaining and Government or State intervention (Chidi, 2017). "Collective bargaining was originated by the Webbs to describe the process of agreeing terms and conditions of employment through representatives of employers (and possibly their associations) and representatives of employees (and probably their unions)" (Rose, 2008, p.274). Organisations in the public sector are owned by the government and are engaged in producing goods and rendering services that satisfy the aspirations and yearnings of the citizens at reasonable or subsidised prices (Chidi, 2017).

Collective bargaining was introduced in the public sector in 1948, under the Whitley councils system which was meant for the regulation of employment conditions in government establishments. In its industrial relations policy, published in 1955 the Nigerian government reaffirmed its confidence in the effectiveness of voluntary negotiation and collective bargaining for the determination of wages (Fashoyin, 1987). According to Fashoyin (1987), for a long time the public employer has used the civil service regulations and *ad-hoc*

London International Conferences, 28-30 January 2021, hosted online by UKEY Consulting and Publishing, London, United Kingdom

wage commissions in determining wages and a host of other conditions of service in the public sector and this has hampered effective collective bargaining in the public sector.

The objective of this paper is to review wages and salaries determination and adjustments in the Nigerian public sector from 1934 to 2014. Other issues discussed are the Labour Act, the Minimum Wage Act, Pension Scheme, the National Health Insurance Scheme as well as the Employees' Compensation Act which regulates payments to employees for injuries/death, health insurance. To achieve this objective, the authors adopted a qualitative research approach and relied on secondary source of data based on the review of literature. The paper is structured into eight sections. Section one is the introductory section. Section two reviews wage commissions in Nigeria. Section three examines the labour Act. The fourth section reviews the employees' compensation Act. Section five examines the minimum wage Act in Nigeria. Section six dwells on the national pension scheme in Nigeria. Section seven reviews the NHIS scheme; while section eight deals with conclusion and recommendations.

2. A Review of Wage Commissions in Nigeria

According to Otobo (2007), the government as an employer of labour has been determining public sector terms and conditions through the establishment and functioning of wages and salaries commissions. There exists now a permanent National Salaries, Incomes and Wages Commission in Nigeria established by Act 99 of 1993. In Nigeria, pay/wage determination via wage commissions dates back to the colonial era with the establishment of the Hunt Commission in 1934. The establishment of the Hunt Commission opened the floodgate for the establishment of several wage commissions such as the Bridges Commission in 1941, Tudor-Davis Commission in 1945, Harragin Commission in 1946, Miller

Commission in 1947, Phillipson Commission and Whitley Commission in 1948. Other Commissions that followed include the Gorsuch Commission of 1955, Mbanefo Commission of 1959, Morgan Commission of 1963/1964, Eldwood Commission of 1966, Adebo Commission of 1970/1971, Udoji Public Service Review Commission of 1974, Akintola Williams Commission of 1975, Onosode Presidential Commission on Parastatals 1981, Cookey Presidential Commission on Salaries and Conditions of Service of University Staff of 1981 and Ademolekan Presidential Commission on Salaries and Conditions of Service of Federal Polytechnics, Colleges of Technology, Advanced Teachers and Technical Colleges Staff of 1981, Dotun Philip Commission of 1985, Fatai Williams Commission of 1990, Ukandi Damachi Commission of 1990, Longe Commission of 1991, Ayida Alison Commission of 1994.

Others are the Report of the Vision 2010 Committee of 1997, Phillip Asiodu Committee on the Review of Academic and Professional Allowances for staff of Federal Universities, Polytechnics and Colleges of Education of 1998/1999. Phillip Asiodu Committee on the Review of Harmonised Salaries and Allowances in the Federal Service And the National Minimum Wage, Shehu Sule/Ason Bur Committee on the review of Professional Allowances for Doctors and other Health Professionals of 2000, Ufot Ekaette Presidential Committee on Monetisation 2002, Pension Reform Commission, 2004, Ernest Shonekan Presidential Committee on the Consolidation of Emoluments in the Public Sector of 2005/2006, Onosode FGN/ASUU Re-Negotiation Committee of 2009, Alfa Belgore Committee of 2009/2010, Minimum Wage Review Under President Good luck Jonathan, 2011.

The foregoing Commissions were set up in the colonial period/era and post-colonial era, by successive governments in Nigeria both military and civilian and their objective is to ensure that employers do not exploit their workers and for employers to pay fair and equitable compensation to Nigerian workers in both the public and private sectors (Ekwoaba & Olusanya, 2014; Ekwoaba & Ideh, 2013). Workers' pay or compensation is regulated through government labour policy as stipulated by the Nigerian labour laws or legislation. These laws include the Labour Act, the Employees' Compensation Act, the Minimum Wage Act, the Pension Act, and the National Health Insurance Act. These are discussed in profundity in what follows:

3. A Review of the Labour Act of 1974

The first set of policies that have important implications for the evolving labour market realities is the reform of certain labour laws that are intended to protect workers in employment. Thus, the primary labour law is the Labour Act of 1974 which has been incorporated into the Laws of the Federation, 1990. Section 7 (1) of the Labour Act, Cap 198, Laws of the Federation of Nigeria 1990 provides that an employee must be given a written letter of appointment within three months of engagement. Such letter should specify, among other things, the date, name and place of work where the worker is engaged, the nature of the employment, whether, for example, work is for a fixed term and when the contract expires. In the event of disengagement, it should state the period of notice by either party. It should also state the hours of work, rate of pay and the periodicity of payment, holiday and provision for sickness or injury and terms relating to these.

The aim of these provisions of the law is that a formal contract of employment should be given to the worker. However, it is an irony that the provisions of this law cover only workers in standard/ regular employment, ostensibly because many workers in non-standard work are engaged informally and often without written contract or letter of employment. In some cases, not only do some employers fail to offer formal

London International Conferences, 28-30 January 2021, hosted online by
UKEY Consulting and Publishing, London, United Kingdom

appointment letters, they do not keep records of those employed, presumably to evade the law. Instances such as these have increased the vulnerability of the affected workers (Fashoyin, Owoyemi & Chidi, 2012).

4. A Review of the Employees' Compensation Act (ECA) of 2010

Since some health bills are still paid by a number of Nigeria employees owing to occupational death, injuries and diseases, the Nigerian government from the colonial era came up with workmen compensation as a way of compensating employees for their loss or injury in the course of employment. Nigerian employees most times do leave employment earlier than retirement as a result of injuries sustained at work or during employment. The colonial government in a bid to ensure that Nigerian workers still maintained their standard and living conditions even with the injuries, enacted the first Workmen Compensation Ordinance in 1941. The Ordinance was sequel to the Trade Union Ordinance of 1938 which gave legal backing for the formation of trade unions in Nigeria. The 1941 Ordinance was followed by the Labour Code Ordinance of 1945. The two Ordinances were to ensure the safety of employees at work. By 1958, the Factory Ordinance was enacted to ensure that factories were registered and that workers security, safety and welfare were provided for at factory premises. In the 1987, both the Factory Act and Workmen Compensation Act were amended to cover not just the provision of safety measures but also compensation for injuries and death sustained in the course of employment.

With the coming of the democratic government in 1999, the Workmen Compensation Act was instituted in 2004. The act was optional to employers who are willing to provide additional cover for employees and was mainly left for the private sectors after its repeal in 2010 as government does not collect fund and neither does it manage the fund for the sector. Government gives the private sector regulations that will help them to choose insurers. Insurance experts have objected to this government stance, stating that no profit-driven public sector can deliver social security (Abubakar, 2011). The flaws associated with the 2004 Workmen Compensation Act led to the establishment of the Employees' Compensation Act of 2010 which was signed into law by President Goodluck Ebele Jonathan in 2011.

The New Employees' Compensation Act (ECA) of 2010, which repealed the 2004 Workmen Compensation Act aims at improving the welfare of Nigerian workers. It introduced a new special security scheme for workers in the country. The Act makes provisions for compensation to employees and their dependants for any death, injury, disease, or disability arising out of or in the course of employment and other related matters. The objective of the Act is to, among other things; make comprehensive provisions for compensation to employees who suffer from occupational diseases or those who sustain injuries arising from accidents that occur at the workplace or in the course of employment. It is intended to bring the system of compensation for employees in line with global best practices and trends. The welfare of employees is of paramount consideration under the Act.

As pointed out earlier, the Employees' Compensation Act of 2010 is a reformulation of the Workmen's Compensation Act of 2004. The new law makes provisions for payment of compensation to employees who suffer from occupational diseases or sustain injuries arising from accident at the workplace or in the course of employment. The law creates, in Section 56(1), the Employees' Compensation Fund into which all contributions by employers shall be lodged, which is to compensate employees or their dependants for any injury, disability, death or disease arising out of or in the course of employment. In section 36(1) of the Act, every employer shall within the first 2 years of the commencement of law, make a minimum monthly contribution of one per cent of the total monthly payroll into the Fund. The Act establishes a contributory compensation fund referred to as the Employee's Compensation Fund managed in the interest of both employers and employees. The Fund is managed by the Nigeria Social Insurance Trust Fund Management Board (the Board) established under the Nigeria Social Insurance Trust Fund Act No. 73 of 1993. Contribution to the Fund derives from various sources including, a take-off grant by the federal government, compulsory contributions, fees and charges assessed to employers, gifts or other grants from local or international organisations, and also earnings from profitable investments of the surplus fund by the Board.

The current employee compensation scheme now recognises new categories of workplace injuries such as mental stress resulting from exceptional circumstances in the course of employment. In addition, the scheme provides rehabilitation for injured employees. The scheme seems to have the effect of easing the burden on employers who will not be required to contribute further to the welfare of an injured employee in the event of any accident or injury, no matter the amount of liability involved. As a general rule, an employee or his dependant is entitled to apply to the Board for compensation within one year after the date of the death, injury or disease arising from an occupational accident or disease. Where special circumstances exist, an application for compensation may be made within three years of the occurrence of the accident or injury for which a claim is being made. Payments of compensation under the Act do not affect the employee's retirement benefit payable under the Pension Reform Act 2004 as amended in 2014. It is a very crucial point to note that for any claim for compensation to be sustained by the employee, the claim must be used for injury arising out of or in the course of employment.

London International Conferences, 28-30 January 2021, hosted online by UKEY Consulting and Publishing, London, United Kingdom

It is significant that the law covers employees in both the public and private sectors of the economy. It also covers self-employed persons, whether in the formal or informal economy. However, members of the Armed Forces, except those employed in a civilian capacity are excluded from the scheme (FRN 2010, Official Gazette). The potential contribution of this innovative law to the welfare of workers is enormous, but it remains to be seen if the operators are able to bring the various categories of employers into its coverage, and perhaps more significantly, whether the enforcement provisions are able to ensure that all employers' categories faithfully implement the revolutionary provisions.

In the Employees' Compensation Act 2010, specifically, employees are liable to compensation for death, injury and disease resulting in the course of work. Compensable categories include death, injury, mental stress, occupational disease, hearing impairment and other injuries occurring outside the normal workplace. Even though there is no judicial pronouncement specifically relating to the Act, previous judicial decisions have attempted to define the phrase "in the course of work". The courts have stated that the "course of the servant's employment can be extended to acts which are outside the employee's working hours and outside the employer's premises, provided the acts are done for the purpose of the employer's business." This definition is consistent with the definition provided in the Act. The Act also provides that an employee shall be entitled to payment of compensation with respect to any accident sustained on the way between the place of work and employee's principal or secondary place of residence; the place where the employee usually takes meals; the place where he/she usually receives remuneration, provided that the employer has a prior notification of such place These are in agreement with ILO Conventions No. 121 on Employment Benefit 1964 and Convention 102 on Social Security (Minimum Standard) 1954.

London International Conferences, 28-30 January 2021, hosted online by UKEY Consulting and Publishing, London, United Kingdom

The provision in the New Act complies with periodic payments as recommended by ILO Convention 121 of 1964. In the case of death of the bread winner or permanent incapacity, the Board makes a periodic payment, specifically on monthly basis, to the dependants of the deceased employee or incapacitated employee. The amounts and conditions of payment may change as follows: Increments in periodical payments are provided if the disabled persons required constant help or attendance of another. The condition of periodic payment can be reviewed, suspended or cancelled depending on changes in the degree of working capacity or substantial changes in the cost of living. The Act makes room for changes in payment based on the degree of incapacity or rate of adjustment of the injured employee; but this is at the discretion of the Board. For example, Part III, No. 7 of the New Employees' Compensation Act stated that the compensation payable for occupational disease may, in addition to the provision of this section of the Act be determined by regulations made by the Board. What this means is that besides the provisions of this Act, the Act also empowers the Board to determine compensation by its regulation. In our opinion, this allows for flexibility of the Act. The minimum benefit levels stipulated by the Act includes: In the case of death resulting from the course of work the scale of compensation is 90 per cent of the total monthly remuneration of the deceased employee as of the date of death where the deceased leaves dependants wholly depending on his earnings, a widow or widower. Part IV, sub-section 1(a) of the Employees' Compensation Act identified the following conditions and the scale of compensation: where the deceased employee leaves dependants wholly dependent on his earnings, a widow or widower:

i. and two or more children, a monthly payment of a sum equal to 90 per cent of the total remuneration of the employee as of the date of death,

London International Conferences, 28-30 January 2021, hosted online by UKEY Consulting and Publishing, London, United Kingdom

ii. and one child, a monthly payment of a sum equal to 85 per cent of the total monthly remuneration of the deceased employee as of the date of death,

iii. without a child who, at the date of death of the employee, is 50 years of age or above, or is an invalid spouse, a monthly payment of a sum equal to 60 per cent of the total monthly remuneration of the deceased employee, and

iv. who, at the date of the death of the employee is not an invalid spouse, in under the age of 50 years and has no dependant children, a monthly payment of a sum that is equal to the product of the percentage determined by subtracting 1 per cent from 60 per cent for each year for which the age of the dependant, at the date of death of the employee, is under the age of 50 years, and provided that total percentage shall not be less than 30 per cent.

5. A Review of the Minimum Wage Act in Nigeria

The minimum wage ensures that all workers receive a predetermined minimum wage (Ujo, 2008). Given the structure of employment and the growing size of non-standard workforce, the role of the minimum wage in serving as a safety net for workers at the lowest rung of the income ladder can hardly be over-emphasised. In fact, this role of the minimum wage in protecting the workers at the lower rung of the income ladder has been one of the outstanding features of wage determination in Nigeria since the 1950s. With growing number of non-standard workforce relative to those in regular or standard employment, the role of the minimum wage in providing regular income for the designated workers is key to the minimisation of poverty in the country. Yet the determination of the minimum wage has for several decades been acrimonious and turbulent aspects of the employment relationship in Nigeria. (For a historical account of the determination of the minimum wage, see Ezeife, 1987: Fashoyin, 1991). Minimum wage covers only the financial aspect of compensation and was not obvious until 1972, when the Nigerian government set the monthly financial compensation of workers at ₦60 minimum per month.

In 1981, following the usual drama and acrimony surrounding the determination of the minimum wage, the government and the social partners agreed to an ad hoc tripartite panel to determine the minimum wage. After threats of strikes for the lack of progress in the negotiations, the parties agreed to a minimum wage of ₦125 per month for the designated workers. Between 1981 and 2010, four such ad hoc tripartite determinations had taken place, at a regularity of 10 year period. The more recent minimum wage determination was concluded in 2010. This exercise, similar to earlier exercises, have drawn considerable acrimony (even at the time of writing), because of the reluctance of state governments to pay, on claims that they had not been duly consulted by the federal government, while they questioned the right of the central government to determine the minimum wage for them.

These procedural issues of the determination of the minimum wage speak only to one of the fundamental anomalies in the determination of the minimum wage in Nigeria. There is the equally and perhaps more fundamental issue relating to the category of workers that ought to be targeted when determining the minimum wage. Historically in Nigeria, the minimum wage has targeted the lowest paid wage earner in the public service, and the corresponding grades in the private sector. However, as has recently been argued, this target is not only a misadventure; it is crisis-laden (Fashoyin, 2011). In the first place, by targeting the bottom of the well-established salary ladder in the public sector, the minimum wage sets off an uncontrollable wage agitation by upper-grades wage earners who justifiably want to maintain existing wage parity between their grades and that of those at the bottom. As Fashoyin (2011) argues, the crisis over the target of the minimum wage policy is inevitable and will subsist as long as the policy fail to focus on those members of the labour force in low wage establishments and who are disadvantaged because they lack organisation or the capacity to influence their wages. In other words, the policy on the minimum wage has ignored the role of the minimum wage as a wage floor designed to protect workers in the bottom of wage income. This point is critical because a growing proportion of the workforce has fallen into the minimum wage category as a result of the observable increase in non-standard employment in the country.

In 1982, there was a salary and wage freeze which was lifted in 1988 fiscal year (UNESCO, 2012). In 1985, the 1st of October to be precise, the General Ibrahim Babangida administration applied deduction of between 2 per cent to 20 per cent from workers' salaries, rents and dividends. The then Head of State, General Ibrahim Babangida told Nigerian workers then that they were giving to their future generation (Babangida, 1991). In 1990, workers' minimum wage rose to ₦250, and by 1993, it was increased to ₦363. In 1998, there was a sharp increase to ₦3,500. In 2000, under the administration of President Olusegun Obasanjo the minimum wage was split into two: with federal government paying its workers ₦7,500 minimum while the states and private employers paid ₦5,500. The Minimum Wage Act of 2004 seems to harmonise minimum wages across federal, state and the private sector. In 2011, the Minimum Wage (Amendment) Act, which replaced the Minimum Wage Act of 2004 was signed into law on the 22nd of March , 2011; by the then President of Nigeria Dr. Goodluck Ebele Jonathan to review the national minimum wage upward from ₦7,500 to ₦18,000 minimum per month.

Till date, the minimum wage which an average Nigerian worker earns monthly statutorily stands at ₦18,000 per month. The minimum wage was increased to ₦18, 000; as against the demand of the NLC for ₦52, 500. Minimum wage has been put in place via legislation. In Nigeria, the law on minimum wage has not been religiously complied with by many state governments in Nigeria owing to inability to pay arising from poor revenue base. As of the time of writing this paper, the price of a bag of rice has almost exceeded the minimum wage of ₦18, 000 per month. The current democratic dispensation under President Muhammadu Buhari has set up a minimum wage committee for the review of the current minimum wage at the instance of organised labour in view of the excruciating economic conditions that Nigerian workers are grappling with. However, it remains to be seen if this committee will come up with a minimum wage of ₦ 56, 000 per month which is the yearning and aspiration of organised labour. As of the time of writing this paper, organised labour has threatened an industrial action twice over the minimum wage as state governments have divergent views on the amount to pay. Just last week, the Federal government gave a tacit approval of ₦30, 000 monthly minimum wage. There is a need to institute the living wage for every employee so that they can live well and have a reasonable standard of living (Chidi, 2017).

6. A Review of the National Pension Scheme

The Nigerian government has equally made substantial adjustments in the non–wage compensation of pension. In explaining the non-wage compensation of pension and the associated reforms; Anyim, Olusanya and Okere (2014), PENCOM (2008), Ahmed, (2006) and Odia and Okoye (2012), view pension as the benefits employers pay to employees on retirement or after attaining the statutory retirement age or age of superannuation, which makes employees to be financially independent at old age and during post-employment years. Though a deferred reward and remuneration package, it guarantees employees comfortable life after active years of service. According to Adams (2005), pension is the amount that company or government pays an employee after having worked for a specific period of time and retires either as a result of ill health, old age or having reached the statutory age of retirement. This amount is assumed to be paid monthly to retirees until their death by employers. Chizueze, Ikeji, Agba and Ogaboh (2011) and Adebayo (2006), view pension as a scheme of an earned income that has employees paying a portion of their earning during their working life into the pension fund. Ozor (2006), posits that the sums paid by employees during their working life can only be earned upon disengagement from active service. Nigerian employees before 2004 Pension Reform Act were scary of the word pension because the scheme was not only problematic but also fragmented and rigid. The scheme caused untold hardship on retirees who have to queue long hours, wait for days, weeks, months and even years to earn their entitlement (Dostal & Cassey, 2007).

The Nigeria pension scheme can be traced to the 20th century organised by workforce in the private and public sectors in the colonial era (Barrow, 2008), Ikeji (2002) as cited in Anyim et al. (2014), opined that the colonial pension law was primarily designed for the British officials who moved from place to place within the vast British Empire and the intention was to guarantee continuity of service wherever they had worked. He further noted that the Pension Ordinance had limited application to Nigerian or indigenous employees and was granted at the pleasure of the Governor-General. This implies that the pension scheme at that period of time was not an automatic right of Nigerians who were discriminated against and did not have equal rights as their British counterparts. The Nigeria first pension scheme which was inaugurated in 1951 with the Pension Ordinance had a retroactive effect from the 1st of January, 1946 (Balogun, 2006; Barrow, 2008). The legislation provided pension and gratuity for public sector employees while the National Provident Fund (NPF) established in 1961 was the first legislation enacted on Pension matters to cover private sector employees (Anyim et al, 2014). The 1961 pension scheme was based on 6 per cent basic salary of 80 shillings (now ₦8) contribution which was shared equally by both employer and employee, that is employer contributes 40 shillings (now ₦4) while employee contributes 40 shillings (now ₦4). Eight naira (₦8) is based on "₦1 to 10 shillings "in line with the Federal Government change to decimal currency policy of Naira and Kobo on the 1st of January, 1973 (CBN, 2015).

The Non-contributory and unfunded pension plan enshrined in Cap.30 of the Laws of the Federation of Nigeria of 1961 is a colonial inheritance which was solely designed to take care of colonial administration employees (Orifowomo, 2006). The 1951 and 1961 Pension Ordinance and National Provident Fund (NPF) were to cater for pension issues in both the public and private sectors. These were followed in 1972 and 1979 by Pension Act No.102 and Pension Act No. 103 which catered for the Armed Forces. Other Pension Acts included, Pension Right of Judges Act No. 5 of 1985, the 1987 Pension Act No. 75 that established the Police and other government agencies pension schemes. The 1987 Pension Art established the Local Government Staff Pension Board which caters for local government employees' pensions (Sule & Ezugwu, 2006 as cited in Ayegba, James & Odoh, 2013).

The challenges of the previous schemes made government to establish the National Social Insurance Trust Fund (NSITF) in 1993 under Decree No. 73, to replace the defunct National Pension Fund (Odia & Okoye, 2012). NSITF which took effect from the 1st of July, 1994; was set up to address pension and retirement issues of employees in the private sector of the economy against any law of employment that is against workers in their old age, invalidity or death (Balogun, 2006). The Pension Act of 1997 allowed parastatals to have different pension arrangements for their staff. The pensions in Nigeria can be classified as follows: retiring pension, compensating pension, superannuating pension and compassionate allowance. The entire pension scheme used in Nigeria from 1951 to 1997 was the Pay- As -You -Go (PAYG) pension policy. The 1951 scheme which has retroactive effective from January 1946 has basic salary contribution of 6 per cent. That is of 3 per cent for the employer and 3 per cent for the employee. Other schemes include: the 1961 National Provident Fund Scheme had 7.5 per cent contribution of basic salary of 2.5 per cent by the employee and 5 per cent by the employer.

The Armed Forces Pension Act No 103 had 15 per cent contribution of basic salary of 12.5per cent by the employer and 2.5 per cent by the employee. The 1976 and 1979 Pension Act No 102 that commenced on the 1st of April, 1974 and the other Government Agencies Pension Act No 75, 1987 and Local Government Pension Decree 1987 had 7.5 per cent basic salary contribution of 2.5 per cent by the employee and 5 per cent by the employer. From 1995 to 1999, the basic contribution rose to between 16.7 per cent and 30 per cent. The percentage contribution was reversed in 2002 to 10 per cent of 3.5 per cent contribution by employee and 6.5per cent by the employer (Fapohunda, 2013; Odia & Okoye, 2012).

In the PAYG scheme, three tiers of government are responsible for the pension of public servants while some corporate organisations, especially the multinationals had special pension programme for employees. The lack of payment after retirement by PAYG Pension schemes otherwise known as ''Benefit Plan'' owing to government budgetary allocations, non-contributory bottlenecks and corruption in terms of misuse and embezzlement of pension fund led to the establishment of the 2004 Pension Scheme otherwise known as the ''Contributory Pension Scheme.'' The 2004 Contributory Pension Scheme, took care of the challenges of budgetary provision release by all tiers of government, fraud and corruption to name a few. According to Ayegba, James and Odoh (2013) and Goloma, (2009), the 2004 Pension Reform Act was to remove the usual delays in processing the retirement benefits of workers in all sectors of the economy. According to Sule and Ezugwu (2009) as well as Ahmed,

(2008), the 2004 Pension Reform came to remove the various problems inherent in the PAYG at both the public and private sectors of the Nigeria economy. Government aims at establishing the Pension Act 2004, invariably was to relieve government of pension problems, reduce the suffering of pensioners and give an average Nigerian employee hope in retirement.

The objectives of the new pension reform are to ensure that every worker receives his/her retirement benefits as and when due, empower the worker, assist workers to save in order to cater for their livelihood during old age, establish uniform rules, regulations and standards for administration of pension matters and establish strong regulatory and supervisory framework for the scheme (Pension Reform Act, 2004). In the 2004 Pension Reform Act, every employee shall maintain a Retirement Savings Account (RSA) in his/her name with any Pension Fund Administrator (PFA) of his/her choice and notify the employer of the details. The scheme is comprised of 15 per cent total contribution with the employee and employer each contributing a minimum of 7.5 per cent of the employee's monthly emoluments of monthly basic salary, transport and housing allowances. In the case of the Armed Forces, 12.5 per cent contribution by the employer, and 2.5 contribution per cent by the employee. The scheme covers all organisations with at least 5 employees in their employment. The Pension Act 2004 was amended in 2014. The 2014 Pension Amendment Act covers organisations with as low as 3 employees and a total of 18 per cent contribution based on emoluments as agreed in contract of employment by both employer and employee. In the 2014 Pension Act Reform, the employer is required to contribute 10 per cent while the employee will make a contribution of 8 per cent of total emolument (Anyim et al, 2014; Fapohunda, 2013).

A holder of a retirement savings account upon retirement and on attaining the age of 50 years, whichever is later shall utilise the balance standing to the credit of his/her retirement saving account for the following benefits: programmed monthly or quarterly withdrawals calculated on the basis of an expected life span; annuity for life purchased from a Life Insurance Company licensed by the National Insurance Commission with monthly or quarterly payment; and lump sum from the balance standing to the credit of his/her retirement savings account; provided that the amount left after that lump sum withdrawal shall be sufficient to procure an annuity or fund programmed withdrawals that can produce an amount not less than 50 per cent of his/her annual remuneration as of the date of his/her retirement. Any employee who retires before the age of 50 years in accordance with the terms and conditions of his/her employment may, on request, withdraw a lump sum of money not more than 25 per cent percent of the amount standing in retirement saving account; provided that such withdrawals shall only be made after six months of such retirement and the retired employee does not secure another employment. Any amount payable as retirement benefits is exempted from tax.

7. A Review of the National Health Insurance Scheme (NHIS)

The non-wage compensation of health insurance which covers employees in both the private and public sectors of the Nigerian economy has also undergone reforms to arrive at its current form. With respect to the Universal Healthcare Coverage (UHC) around the world, the World Health Organisation (WHO) in its report observed that it has been difficult to achieve universal healthcare coverage in many developing countries owing to out-of-pocket expenses which include over the counter payments for medicines and fees for consultations and procedure (World Health Organisation Report, 2010). Medical fees especially have been the main challenge to health care coverage and utilisation; not just for employees but also for the entire population of most developing countries and Nigeria is no exception. Health facilities are inadequate and the cost of accessing health care is expensive in Nigeria (Yohesor, 2004; Odeyemi & Nixon, 2013; Vonke & Sunday, 2014).

The yearly budgetary national allocation to health in Nigeria has not only been fluctuating but has been meagre to cater for the health needs of its over 160 million people. This is evident in the report of the Budget Office of the Federation and the Federal Ministry of Finance in 2012. The report of the Budget Office for year 2000, shows that ₦15.7 billion which is 2.1 per cent of the national budget was allocated to the health sector. This was increased to ₦42.6 billion in 2001, representing 271 per cent increase to 2000 and 4.1per cent of total annual budget. In 2002, it was ₦44.7 billion and 1.9 per cent of annual budget for that year. In 2003, increased to ₦52.2 billion and 2.1 per cent of annual budget. In 2004 the health budget was ₦59.8 and 1.9 per cent of total annual budget. The year 2005, witnessed the allocation of ₦71.7 billion, representing 3.2 per cent of the annual budget. In 2006 health budget increased to ₦106.9 billion and 5.6 per cent of total annual budget. In the following years: 2007, 2008 and 2009 the health budgets stood at ₦122.9 billion, ₦143.9 billion and ₦154.6 billion respectively representing 5.1 per cent, 3.6 per cent and 4.3 per cent of the total annual budgets for the three consecutive years. In 2010 and 2011, budgetary allocations to health stood at ₦164.9 billion and ₦266.7 billion respectively which is 3.7 per cent and 5.4 per cent of total annual budgets for the two consecutive years. From the foregoing therefore, it is crystal clear that successive governments' budgetary allocations to health have been very inadequate to cater for the health needs of its huge population. The only way out of this quagmire is for government to encourage the risk–pooling prepayment approach as exemplified by the National Health Insurance Scheme (NHIS) to cater for the health compensation of the country's workforce (Onyebede, Goyit & Nnadi, 2012; NHIS Report, 2005; World Health Organisation Report, 2010).

The idea of Health Bill on National Health Insurance Scheme in Nigeria is not new phenomenon; it was conceived in 1960 under the Halevy's Committee on Lagos Health Bill. But not until 1984, did National Council on Health, set up a committee to advise government on it owing to legislative issues and political instability. The Committee did not start review until 1985, when they did review, the health sector advised that the National Health Insurance Scheme bill be kick started. The bill was not promulgated until 1997 when the government of the Federal Republic of Nigeria in response to the World Health Organisation (WHO) clarion call, repackaged and launched the Nigerian National Health Insurance Scheme on the 15th of October, 1997. The scheme had no enabling law establishing it, until the promulgation of Decree 35 otherwise now referred to as Act 35 of 1999 in May 1999. The health reform was in essence stalled between 1960 and 1997 by legislation and political instability in the country. The scheme only became reactivated on the 6th of June, 2005, after another 6 years of delay (NHIS Report, 2005). The objective of the National Health Insurance Scheme was to give good health care services, reduce medical bills, give equal health care cost among different income groups, and employees in both the public and private sectors of the economy.

The NHIS which is an agency under the Federal Ministry of Health consist of three main programmes: one formal and two informal (Odeyemi & Nixon, 2013). The Formal Sector Social Health Insurance Programme (FSSHIP) covers public employees and the Organised Private Sector (OPS) employees, and is implemented via a managed care model funded through percentage contributions from employees and employers. The scheme has contributory premium of 15 per cent of worker's basic salary with the employee contributing 5 per cent and the employer contributing 10 per cent. It is mandatory for

London International Conferences, 28-30 January 2021, hosted online by UKEY Consulting and Publishing, London, United Kingdom

organisations with ten or more employees (Metiboba 2011, NHIS 2012, Odeyemi & Nixon, 2013). The two other schemes, the Urban Self-Employed Social Health Insurance Programme (USSHIP) and the Rural Community Social Health Insurance Scheme (RCSHIP) are outside the formal sector and not part of the focus of this paper. As a compensation package, the NHIS which collects premium purchases health services that cover the illness of employees, their spouses and four children under the age of 18 (NHIS, 2005). According to Ichocku (2005), Yohesor (2004), and Metibuba (2011), despite the NHIS, exorbitant health services bills are still paid for by employees as the scheme does not cover high cost illnesses such as surgery, hypertension, dental problems to name a few. Only generic drugs are given to employees, spouses and children under the age of 18. In most cases, the Health Maintenance Organisations (HMOs) lack essential drugs thereby leading to additional financial burdens on the employees who bear the cost of recommended medications which are in some cases are exorbitant.

8. Conclusion and Recommendations

This paper set out to examine wages and salaries determination as well as adjustments in the Nigerian public sector from 1934 to 2014. It has been observed that the use of *ad-hoc* wage commissions in the determination of wages and a host of other conditions of service in the public sector has hampered effective collective bargaining in the public sector. Workers' pay or compensation is regulated through government labour policy as stipulated by the Nigerian labour laws or legislation. The provisions of these labour policies have both positive and negative implications for the Nigerian workers. These laws include the Labour Act, the Employees' Compensation Act, the Minimum Wage Act, the Pension Act, and the National Health Insurance Act. These public policies have been used in the determination and adjustments of wages and salaries in the

Nigerian public sector. A cursory examination of these policies reveals that their provisions tend to benefit workers in the formal sector. Although, an x-ray of the policies reveal that workers in the informal economy are covered by the provisions of some of these lofty public policies, but from experience, the workers in the informal economy have been relegated to the background and are yet to fully benefit from the provisions of these public policies. With respect to the provisions of the Labour Act, there have been instances where letters of employment were not issued to workers even after the three months mandatory period specified in the Act. This is preponderant in the informal economy/sector. The minimum wage of ₦18,000 per month is meagre considering the high cost of living in Nigeria at the moment. With regard to the administration of pension, a lot needs to be done to ensure a hitch-free payment of pension to retirees as and when due. The NHIS seems to be for the very few workers in the formal sector as well as those in the urban centres/ cities. Those in the informal sector and rural areas have not been fully covered.

The authors hereby recommend that the NHIS should be expanded to accommodate workers in the informal sector and those in the rural areas for the impact to be more felt and visible. It is also recommended that the adoption of collective bargaining and the commitment on the part of the government to abide by the ensuing agreement with unions in the public sector is the surest means for promoting peaceful labour-government relations and to a large extent forestall incessant strikes that have bedevilled the public sector in recent times. There is the need for the Ministry of Labour and Employment to be alive to its responsibilities by ensuring that government labour policies and laws are implemented to the letter. There is the urgent need to step up labour administration and inspection by the Ministry. With regard to the embezzlement of pension funds, there should be stiff penalties imposed on those who mismanage or embezzle such funds and the penalty should be life imprisonment or capital punishment. On the issue of health for employees and Nigerians in general, robust budgetary allocations should be allotted to the health sector every year to meet the health needs of workers and Nigerians. In the same vein, the state-of-the-art medical facilities and centres should be established in the six geo-political zones to meet the health needs of the teeming Nigerians to reduce medical tourism abroad. This of course will assist to conserve foreign exchange which can be ploughed back to the economy for developmental projects that will benefit the citizenry.

References

Abubakar, U.M. (2011). Why insurance industry lost workmen's compensation Act. *Vanguard Newspaper*, www.vanguardngr.com.

Adams, R.A. (2005). *Public sector accounting and finance.* Lagos: Corporate Publisher Ventures.

Adebayo, Y.K. (2006). *Essentials of human resources management*. Benin City: Weliscops Services.

Ahmed, M.K. (2006). The contributory pension scheme. Institutional and legal framework. *CBN Bullion, 30* (2), 1-18

Ahmed, M.K. (2008). Pension reform in Nigeria: Transitions from the defined benefits to defined contribution. *A Paper Presented at the LOPS Workshop on Pension Supervision in Dakar Senegal*, on February 5th.

Anyim, F.C., Olusanya O.A., & Okere, S.A. (2014). A critique of the pension reform Act, 2004 in Nigeria, *Journal of Arts and Humanities, 3*(7), 28-37.

Ayegba, O., James, I. & Odoh, L. (2013). An evaluation of pension administration in Nigeria. *British Journal of Arts and Social Science. 15* (11), 97-108.

Babangida, I.B. (1991). Economic reconstruction and political transition. In I.B. Babangida (Ed.). *For their Tomorrow we gave our Today* (pp.82-109). Lagos: Safari Books.

Balogun, A. (2006). Understanding the new Pension Reform Act (PRA, 2004), *CBN Bullion 30*(2).

Barrow, G. (2008). *Pension fund administration in Nigeria.* Abuja, Nigeria: Pen and Pages Ltd.

Chidi, O.C. (2017). Collective bargaining and salary adjustments in the Nigerian public sector: Contemporary issues and challenges. The *Nigerian Journal of Business and Social Sciences, 10*(1), 19-43.

CBN (2015). *History of Nigeria currency*. www.cbn.gov.ng/currency/historycur.asp.

Chizueze, C., Ikeji, N., Agbe, U.W & Ogaboh, A.M. (2011). Contributory pension scheme, and workers commitment, retention, and attitude towards retirement in Nigerian civil service. *Global Journal of Management and Business Research, 11*(4), 50-60.

Dostal, J.M & Cassey, B.H. (2007). Pension reforms in Nigeria; how not to learn from others. *A Paper Presented at the 57th Political Studies Association, Annual Conference*. Lagos Nigeria. April 11-13

Ekwoaba, J.O., & Olusanya, O.A. (2014). National minimum wage (Amendment) Act 2011: Implication for the Nigerian labour market. *A Paper Presented at the 1st International Conference on Business, Law and Economics organized* by Athens Institute for Education and Research, held at Athens Greece between 5-8th May, 2014. www.athensinstituteforeducationandresearch.org.

Ekwoaba J.O., & Ideh, D.A. (2013). Flexible working arrangement and employees' retention at Nigeria bottling company plc. *A Paper Presented at the International Conference on Management and Business Research organized* by the Society of Technical and Management Professionals (STMP), Gwalior, Madhya Pradesh, India, 23rd-24th November. www.societyofrechinicalandmanagementprofessionals. org.

Employees' Compensation Act, 2010. Federal Republic of Nigeria Offical Gazzette. www.emplyeecompensationact2010.gov.ng

Ezeife, C.P. (1991). National incomes policy and bargaining in the public sector. In T. Fashoyin (Ed.). *Collective Bargaining in the Public Sector in Nigeria* (pp. 101-102). Lagos: Macmillan

Fapohunda, T.M. (2013). The pension system and retirement planning in Nigeria. Mediterranean *Journal of Social Science, 4*(2), 25-34.

Fashoyin, T. (1987). Collective bargaining in the public sector: Retrospect and prospects. In T. Fashoyin (Ed.). *Collective bargaining in the public sector in Nigeria* (pp.1-21). Lagos: Macmillan Nigeria Publishers Ltd.

Fashoyin, T. (1991). Collective bargaining in the public sector in developing countries: The case of Nigeria. *Journal of Collective Negotiations, 20* (2), 101-117.

Fashoyin, T. (1992). *Industrial relations in Nigeria: Development and practice.* (2ⁿᵈed.). Lagos: Longman Nigeria PLC.

Fashoyin, T. (2011). The dynamics of national minimum wage: Lessons from global best practice. *Annual Public Lecture of the Chartered Institute of Personnel Management of Nigeria. Lagos 24 November.*

Fashoyin, T., Owoyemi, O., & Chidi, O.C. (2012). *Non-standard work, collective bargaining and social dialogue in Nigeria.* An ILO Commissioned Project, Geneva

Federal Republic of Nigeria (FRN) (2010). *Official gazette*

Goloma, A.M. (2009). Determination of retirement benefits in the public sector. *The Certified National Accountant. 17*(4). 5-8.

Ichoku, H. (2005). Income redistributive effects of the health care financing system in Nigeria. Retrieved from http://www.meetings&wokshops/DAKAR/restricted/PDFFile/Hyacinthementa

Metiboba S. (2011). Nigeria's national health insurance scheme: The need for beneficiary participation. *Research Journal of International Studies, 22,* 51–56

National Insurance Commission Code (2009). NAICOM code of corporate governance for the Insurance Industry. Retrieved from www.naicomgov.ng.

National Pension Commission (PENCOM) (2008). Code of corporate governance for licensed pension operators. www.pencomgov.ng

NHIS Report (2005). Standard treatment guidelines and referral protocol for primary health care providers. Available at ww.nhis.gov.ng/index.php?option=com

Odeyemi, I.A.O., & Nixon, J. (2013). Assessing equity in the health care through the national health insurance scheme (NHIS) of Nigeria and Ghana: A review based comparative analysis. *International Journal for Equity in Research, 12*(9), 1-8.

Odia, J.O., & Okoye, A.E. (2012). Pension reform in Nigeria: A comparison between the old and the new scheme. *Afro Asian Journal of Social Sciences, 3* (31), 1-17.

Onyebede, K.I., Goyit, M.G., & Nnadi, N.E. (2012). An evaluation of the national health insurance scheme (NHIS) in Jos, a north-central Nigerian city. *Global Advanced Research Journal of Microbiology, 1*(1), 5-12; Available online at http://garjm/index.htm.

Orifowomo, O. A. (2006). A critical appraisal of pension system reforms in Nigeria. *Gonzaga Journal of International Law*, 10, 165-200. Available online at http://www.gonzagajil.org.

Otobo, D. (2007). Contemporary industrial relations in Nigeria. In G. Wood & C. Brewster (Eds.) *Industrial relations in Africa* (pp. 162-181). New York: Palgrave Macmillan

Ozor, E. (2006). Review of factors that slows down the processing of retirement benefits. *A Paper Presented at Chartered Institute of Secretaries and Administration of Nigeria Workshop*, held at Modotel, Enugu. 14th-16th May

Pension Reform Act (2004). *The federal republic of Nigeria official gazette.* Lagos: FGN

Pension Reform Act, (2004). National pension commission. www.pencom.gov.ng.

Pencom (2006): The future of pension management in Nigeria. *A paper presented by the National Pension Commission for the Nigerian South African Chamber of Commerce* on Tuesday 22 August

Rose, E.D. (2008). *Employment relations* (3rd ed.). London: Pearson Education Ltd.

Sule, K.O., & Ezugwu, C.I. (2009). Evaluation of the application of the contributory pension scheme on employee retirement benefits of quoted firms in Nigeria. *African Journal of Accounting, Economics, Finance and Banking Research, 4(4)*, 47-60

The Nigeria National Minimum Wage Act 2011.

Ujo, A.A. (2008). *Understanding public sector personnel administration in Nigeria* (2nd ed.). Kaduna-Nigeria: Joyce Graphic Printers and Publishers.

UNESCO, (2012). Nigeria Project for Revitalization of TVE in Nigeria; Instructional and Teaching Materials. www.unesco-nigeriatve.org/teaching%20material/acc/accountancy/semester2/bfn%20121%20elementof%20banking%20/week10.htm

Vonke, D. & Sunday, B. (2014). The role of national health insurance scheme (NHIS) on the health care demand in Jos central, Nigeria. *Journal of Social Science and Public Policy, 6 (1)*, 122-137

World Health Organisation Report (2010). *The world health report 2010- Health system, improving performance.* Geneva: W.H.O. www.who.org.

London International Conferences, 28-30 January 2021, hosted online by UKEY Consulting and Publishing, London, United Kingdom

Yoder, D., & Staudohar, P. D. (1982). *Personnel management and industrial relations* (7th ed.). Englewood Cliffs, N. J: Prentice-Hall Inc.

Yoshesor, A. (2004). *Social health insurance scheme that works. Recommendation to NHIS.* Abuja: Vast Communication Publishers.

London International Conferences

londonic.uk

ukeyconsultingpublishing.co.uk

Theory and Practice of the Unified tax: Innovation in Taxation

Konstantin P. Taushanzhi
Comrat State University
taushanzhi@mail.ru

S. I. Anastasov
Comrat State University

Abstract

In the present article the essence of the "single tax" (EH) as a new ideology in the economic relationship in the marketplace. The essence of the new paradigm in taxation is based on mutual trust, government and business, which is secured by contractual obligations. The effectiveness of the new tax system was tested in an experiment at a furniture factory "Goliat-Vita".

Keywords: Unified tax, economic experiment, tax treaty, innovation, social contract, anticorruption mechanism, e "shadow economy".

London International Conferences, 28-30 January 2021, hosted online by UKEY Consulting and Publishing, London, United Kingdom

London International Conferences

londonic.uk ukeyconsultingpublishing.co.uk

Police Officers' Opinion on Their Work

R. Malini
PG Department of Commerce and Research Centre,
Sri Parasakthi College for Women, Courtallam
maliniramu@yahoo.co.in

E. Shanmugapriya
PG Department of Commerce and Research Centre,
Sri Parasakthi College for Women, Courtallam
dharshan0689@gmail.com

Abstract

The aim of this study is to find out the opinion of police officers on their working time, nature of work and working environment. Primary data were obtained from 450 police officers working in Tamil Nadu by adopting stratified random sampling techniques to attain the objective. The police officers' opinion was analysed by comparing the total scores with Neutral score. Besides, 'Z' test was applied to test the significant difference in the mean opinion scores of the different categories of the police officers on their work. The police officers opined that they have no fixed lunch time, long working hours. The majority of the police officers (73.33%) strongly agreed the statement "Stress is inherent in police work". They opined that they aware of risks and hazards of their work environment". It is interesting to note that they find their unpleasant work environment as a challenging task. To cope up with stress, the police officer should adopt any stress

London International Conferences, 28-30 January 2021, hosted online by UKEY Consulting and Publishing, London, United Kingdom

R. Malini
E. Shanmugapriya

management technique as they wish. It is suggested that they should practice Yoga and Meditation even though they have stretched schedule. Apart from this police department should arrange tour or some entertainment activity regularly to relieve the police officer to get relax and refresh themselves from their routine work.

Keywords: Work Stress, Police, Police Department.

London International Conferences, 28-30 January 2021, hosted online by UKEY Consulting and Publishing, London, United Kingdom

1. Introduction

Work is an integral part of everyday life, as it is our livelihood or career or business. On an average we spent twelve hours daily life and it is the one third of our entire life. The work environment leads to satisfaction, or conversely stresses to the employees. The police officers are not an exception to this. Police officers generally have to deal with complex problem like murder, mugging and robbery. These issues should be handled by the police officers with the constraints of irregular working hours, lack of holidays, hierarchic pressure and pact with anti-social element. In dealing with these issues, police comes across many children and women involved in these activities both as victims and as offender. It demands more patient, courage and tackling techniques from police.

Hence, Policing is considered to be one of the most masculinized occupations of the World. But the opinion of different categories of the police officers regarding working time, nature and environment varies on the basis of gender, experience and designation. In this context it is essential to know the opinion of different categories of the police officers regarding their work in the traditionally male dominated and predominated career like policing. The good opinions of police officers are essential to equip and develop the work force of Tamil Nadu police department.

Objectives

- To find out the opinion of police officers on their working time, nature of work and working environment.
- To test the significant difference in the means opinion scores of the different categories of the police officers.

2. Research methodology

Source: Both primary and secondary data were used for the study. The primary data were collected from the Police officers working in Tamil Nadu. The primary data was collected through a Questionnaire. The secondary data was collected from annual records, guidelines, brochures, and evaluation report maintained by the Police Department.

Sample design: The researchers have adopted Stratified Random Sampling technique to collect the data.

Sample size: The sample respondents consist of 450 Middle Level Police Officers in Tamil Nadu.

3. Review related to the study

The National and International review related to this study were reviewed and few of them are given below.

Miller *et al* (2009) were analyzed the predictors of job satisfaction among police officers and found experience, job characteristics, autonomy and appraisal system are the important factors in predicting job satisfaction.

Carlan (2007)2 found social contribution, pay, adventure, excitement, autonomy, peer respect, and job security has direct positive effect on the job satisfaction among the police constables.

Kanchana et al (2012)3 found that age, educational qualification, salary, family size and experience are the significant factors influenced the job satisfaction.

Gyamfi (2014)4 was found that physical environment, role ambiguity, work overload, lack of superior support and coworker support leads to high stress among the police officers and arises out of these factors has positive significant influence on their satisfaction towards their job. The author suggested leadership of Police administration should pay much attention to the psychological and physiological needs of their police officers to improve upon the job satisfaction among the officers.

4. Discussion

R. Malini
E. Shanmugapriya

Table 1. Police Officers' Opinion on Working Time

Statements	SA	A	N	D	SD	Total Score	Rank
I have irregular and unpredictable working hours	13 (2.88)	236 (52.44)	161 (35.77)	21 (4.66)	19 (4.22)	1553	IX
Time pressure to complete work	1 (0.22)	18 (4.00)	16 (3.55)	285 (63.33)	130 (28.88)	1875	IV
The working time schedule is outside the control of the worker	7 (1.55)	30 (6.66)	60 (13.33)	209 (46.44)	144 (32.00)	1803	VII
I am unable to take sufficient breaks	3 (1.00)	42 (9.33)	31 (6.88)	249 (55.33)	125 (27.77)	1896	III
My working time can be flexible	165 (36.66)	202 (44.88)	54 (12.00)	27 (6.00)	2 (0.44)	1851	V
I am pressured to work long hours	3 (1.00)	36 (8.00)	36 (8.00)	157 (34.88)	218 (48.44)	1901	II
Working hour involve distraction	3 (1.00)	55 (12.22)	44 (9.77)	142 (31.55)	206 (45.77)	1843	VI
I work for long hours, on overtime and even on holidays	19 (4.22)	225 (50.00)	183 (40.66)	3 (1.00)	20 (4.44)	1570	VIII
There is no fixed lunch time during heavy working hours	4 (1.00)	23 (5.11)	18 (4.00)	105 (23.33)	300 (66.66)	2024	I

Source: Primary Data (Figures in Parentheses are Percentages). Neutral Score: 450*3=1350

It is clear from the Table 1 the highest score is given to the statement "There is no fixed lunch time during heavy working hours". The second rank is given to the statement "I am pressured to work long hours". The third rank is given to the statement "I am unable to take sufficient breaks". The fourth rank is given to the statement "Time pressure to complete work". The fifth rank is given to the statement "My working time can be flexible". The sixth rank is given to the statement "Working hours involves distractions". The seventh rank is given to the statement "The working time schedule is outside the control of the worker". The eighth rank is given to the statement "I work for long hours, on overtime and even on holidays". The last rank is given to the statement "I have irregular and unpredictable working hours". Only 52.44 per cent and 2.88 per cent of the police officers strongly agreed and agreed the statement because the first rank is given to the statement there is no fixed lunch time during heavy working hours.

It is clear from the Table 1 that the police officers agreed that they have unpredictable long working hours without sufficient breaks, lunch time. Besides their working hour involve distraction and outside the control. It is proved by the total scores. All the total scores are above the neutral value (1350). The means, standard deviations and 'Z' values of different categories of the police officers regarding their working time are given in Table 2.

Table 2. "Z" Test on Opinions Scores of Police Officers on Working Time

Factors	Categories	N	Mean	SD	Z
Gender	Male	376	16.5	2.99	0.62
	Female	74	16.83	4.23	
Designation	Gazetted Officers	45	16.91	2.78	0.74
	Non- Gazetted Officers	405	16.53	3.28	
Experience	Senior Police Officers	258	17.10	2.97	4.04*
	Super Senior Police Officers	192	15.85	3.43	

Source: Primary Data. *Z Value is significant at 5% level

It is inferred from the Table 2 that the mean opinion score (16.83) of the female police officers regarding working time is slightly higher than their counterparts (16.51). But, the results of "Z" test reveals that (0.62) there is no significant difference in the mean opinion scores of male and female police officers regarding the working time. It indicates that, irrespective of the gender the police officers have the same opinion on working time.

There is a minor variation in the mean opinion scores of the gazetted officers (16.91) and the non-gazetted officers (16.53). The computed "Z" value of 0.74 indicates that there is no significant difference between the mean opinion scores of the gazetted officers and non-gazetted officers.

Further, the Table 2 shows that the mean opinion score of the senior police officers (17.10) is more than that of those super senior police officers (15.85). The "Z" value of 4.04 shows that there is a significant difference in the mean values of these two groups.

Nature of Work

Police officers work involves prevention, detection and investigation of criminal activity. They are assigned specific task or geographic area on an assigned shift. The natures of work have a direct bearing on stress. Hence, police officer's opinion on nature of work analyses in Table 3.

It is clear from the Table 3 that the highest score is given to the statement "Stress inherent in police work". The second rank is given to the statement "I have to do some work unwillingly due to certain group/political pressure". The third rank is given to the statement "Some assignments are quite risky and complicated". The fourth rank is given to the statement "Personal stresses typically affect members of this profession". The fifth rank is given to the statement "I am placed at remote places for banthopast which is denied of basic amenities".

Table 3. Police Officers' Opinion on Nature of Work

London International Conferences, 28-30 January 2021, hosted online by UKEY Consulting and Publishing, London, United Kingdom

Statements	SA	A	N	D	SD	Total Score	Rank
Stress inherent in police work	330 (73.33)	14 (3.11)	30 (6.66)	72 (16.00)	4 (1.00)	2060	I
I have to do some work unwillingly due to certain group/ political pressure	13 (2.88)	21 (4.66)	28 (6.22)	162 (36.00)	226 (50.22)	1917	II
Some assignments are quite risky and complicated	2 (0.44)	49 (10.88)	57 (12.66)	191 (42.44)	151 (33.55)	1790	III
The working conditions is conducive to learn and reach perfection	120 (26.66)	184 (40.88)	73 (16.22)	65 (14.44)	8 (1.77)	1693	VII
The working condition encourages involve in accomplishing the job	150 (33.33)	150 (33.33)	63 (14.00)	75 (16.66)	12 (2.66)	1701	VI
Rare opportunities for job enrichment, job rotation, job enlargement	23 (5.11)	181 (40.22)	50 (11.11)	141 (31.33)	55 (12.22)	1374	XI
Getting witness is very difficult	3 (1.00)	217 (48.22)	188 (41.77)	10 (2.22)	35 (7.77)	1502	IX
Inability to resolve and close many communal problems	30 (6.66)	125 (27.77)	59 (13.11)	186 (41.33)	50 (11.11)	1451	X
The consequences of work is serious	30 (6.66)	85 (18.88)	27 (6.00)	146 (32.44)	162 (36.00)	1675	VIII
I am placed at remote places for banthopast which is denied of basic amenities	11 (2.44)	92 (20.44)	31 (6.88)	123 (27.33)	193 (42.88)	1745	V
Personal stresses typically affect members of this profession	10 (2.22)	83 (18.44)	33 (7.33)	109 (24.22)	215 (47.77)	1786	IV

Source: Primary Data (Figures in Parentheses are Percentages).
Neutral Score: 450*3=1350

The sixth rank is given to the statement "The working condition encourages involve in accomplishing the job". The

London International Conferences, 28-30 January 2021, hosted online by UKEY Consulting and Publishing, London, United Kingdom

seventh rank is given to the statement "The working condition is conducive to learn and reach perfection". The eighth rank is given to the statement "The consequence of work is serious". The ninth rank is given to the statement "Getting witness is very difficult". The tenth rank is given to the statement "Inability to resolve and close many communal problems". The last rank is given to the statement "Rare opportunities for job enrichment, job rotation, and job enlargement". Only 40.22% and 5.11% of the police officers have strongly disagreed and disagreed the statement.

It is clear from the Table 3 that the police officers opined that "Stress is inherent in police work". It is proved by the total scores. All the total scores are above the neutral value (1350). 'Z' test is applied to find whether there is any significant difference in the mean opinion scores of the different categories of the police officers on nature of work. The police officers mean opinion scores on the basis of Gender, Designation and Experience are given in the Table 4 along with "Z" values.

It is inferred from the Table 4 that the mean opinion score of the female police officers is slightly higher (24.76) than the male police officers (23.92). The result of "Z" test shows that there is no significant difference between the mean opinion scores between the male and female police officers regarding the nature of work. The study reveals that irrespective of gender the police officers have same opinion on nature of work.

London International Conferences, 28-30 January 2021, hosted online by UKEY Consulting and Publishing, London, United Kingdom

Table 4. "Z" Test on Opinions Scores of Police Officers on Nature of Work

Factors	Categories	N	Mean	SD	Z
Gender	Male	376	23.92	3.79	
	Female	74	24.76	5.20	1.32
Designation	Gazetted Officers	45	21.30	3.54	3.72*
	Non-Gazetted Officers	405	24.36	4.01	
Experience	Senior Police Officers	258	23.65	3.68	2.41*
	Super Senior Police Officers	192	24.61	4.49	

Source: Primary Data. *Z Value is significant at 5% level

Non-Gazetted officers mean opinion score (24.36) is greater than the Gazetted officers mean opinion score (21.30). The computed "Z" value (3.72) proves that there is a significant difference between the means of the opinion scores of the Gazetted officers and Non-Gazetted officers.

The super senior police officers and senior police officers have scored the mean opinion scores of 24.61and 23.65 respectively. The computed "Z" value of 2.41 proves that there is a significant difference in the mean opinion scores of the super senior police officers regarding the nature of work.

Working Environment

Police department is one of the important departments for societal wellbeing. Police have to work round the clock to keep public safe. Throughout the day they are doing a restless job. They don't have weekend holiday and occasional holiday. In fact, on those days they have to work even harder in the name of banthopast which leads to frustration. Table 5 shows that the police officers' opinion on working environment.

Table 5. Police Officers Opinion on Working Environment

Statements	SA	A	N	D	SD	Total Score	Rank
I am aware of the risks and hazards of my work environment	33 (7.33)	19 (4.22)	32 (7.11)	129 (28.66)	237 (52.66)	1868	I
Over crowed work environment or work isolation	6 (1.33)	97 (21.55)	66 (14.66)	183 (40.66)	98 (21.77)	1620	IV
Critical incidents from shootings to mass disasters	17 (3.77)	67 (14.88)	45 (10.00)	173 (38.44)	148 (32.88)	1718	III
I find my work environment unpleasant, but it is challenging	14 (3.11)	78 (17.33)	47 (10.44)	136 (30.22)	175 (38.88)	1730	II

Source: Primary Data. (Figures in Parentheses are Percentages). Neutral Score: 450*3=1350

It is clear from the Table 5 the highest score is given to the statement "I am aware of the risks and hazards of my work environment". The second rank is given to the statement "I find my work environment unpleasant". The third rank is given to the statement "Critical incidents from shootings to mass disasters". The last rank is given to the statement "Over crowed work environment of work isolation". The work environment of police officers is complicated and critical. But the police officers felt that it is challenging. It is proved by highest score (1730). The means, standard deviations and 'Z' values of the police officers regarding their work environment are given in Table 6.

London International Conferences, 28-30 January 2021, hosted online by UKEY Consulting and Publishing, London, United Kingdom

Table 6. "Z" Test on Opinions Scores of Police Officers on Work Environment

Factors	Categories	N	Mean	SD	Z
Gender	Male	376	8.47	2.73	1.18
	Female	74	9.08	4.27	
Designation	Gazetted Officers	45	7.30	2.28	3.78*
	Non- Gazetted Officers	405	8.71	3.09	
Experience	Senior Police Officers	258	8.15	2.78	3.41*
	Super Senior Police Officers	192	9.15	3.28	

Source: Primary Data. *Z Value is significant at 5% level.

It is inferred from the Table 6 that the mean opinion score of female police officers is slightly higher than (9.08) the male police officers (8.47). The "Z" value of (1.18) indicates that there is no significant difference between the mean scores of male and female police officers regarding the work environment.

The Non-Gazetted officers of mean score 7.30 is greater than the Gazetted officers means score 8.71. The "Z" value 3.78 shows that there is a significant difference between the mean scores of Gazetted officers and Non-Gazetted officers regarding the work environment.

The super senior police officers have better mean opinion score (8.15) than their counterparts (9.15). The "Z" value of (3.41) indicates that there is a significant difference between the mean opinion scores of the super senior police officers regarding the working environment.

6. Findings

Working Hours

Police officers agreed that they had unpredictable long working hours without sufficient breaks and lunch time. Besides their working hour is out off their control and involve distraction. "Z" test proved that irrespective of the gender and designation police officers had satisfied opinion on working time. But the police officers' opinion about working time varies on the basis of experience.

Nature of Work

Police officers agreed that the stress is inherent in police work. 'Z' test proved that irrespective of the gender police officers had satisfied opinion on nature of work. The police officers with different designation and experience had different opinion on nature of work.

Working Environment

Working environment of police officers is complicated and critical. But the police officers felt that it is challenging. 'Z' test proved that irrespective of the gender police officer had satisfied opinion on work environment. The police officers with different designation and experience had different opinion on work environment.

Police is considered one of the major stressed occupations because of the major stressed occupations because of the irregular working hours, lack of holidays, hierarchic pressure and deal with anti-social element.

7. Suggestions

1.   The basic amenities should be provided when the police officers are placed at remote areas for banthopast.
2.   To cope up with stress, the police officer should adopt any stress management technique as they wish.

London International Conferences, 28-30 January 2021, hosted online by UKEY Consulting and Publishing, London, United Kingdom

3. It is suggested that they should practice yoga and Meditation even though they have stretched schedule.

4. The Tamil Nadu police department should arrange tour or some entertainment activity regularly to relieve the police officer to get relax and refresh themselves from their routine work.

8. Conclusion

Job stress present in all sorts of jobs. Stress among the police officials is common across all the police force of the world. The result of the study also proved that the majority of the police officers (73.33%) strongly agreed that "Stress is inherent in police work". "Prevention is better than cure" based on these idioms the police officers should understand the difficult situation they should be well preferred to face the situation. Many choose this job, ignoring the levels of stress, due to the immense love and respect towards the job. Thus, by overcoming the various types of stress, one would not only make a better career, but also contribute to make a better nation.

References

Carlan (2007). The search for job satisfaction: A survey of Alabama policing", American Journal of Criminal Justice.

G Rajesh Kumar (2009). Dr S Raja Mohan "Work Stress for Traffic Police in Chennai City", Journal of Contemporary Research in Management.

Gyamfi (2014). "Influence of Job Stress on Job Satisfaction: Empirical Evidence from Ghana Police Service", International Business Research.

Miller et al (2009). "Predictors of job satisfaction among police officers: Does personality matter?", Journal of Criminal Justice, September 37(5):419-426.

Police Officer – Nature of Work, Issued 10/77.

Rashmi Hunnuret et al. (2014). Work Place Stress-Causes of Work Place Stress in Police Department: A Proposal for Stress Workplace, IQSR Journal of Business Management (IQSR-JBM), 16(3), 39-47.

https://books.google.co.in/books?isbn=3319145029

https://www.thebalance.com

https://en.oxfortdictionaries.com>authority

http://www.whatishumanresource.com

http://www.tnpolice.gov.in

http://www.ijip.in

londonic.uk   ukeyconsultingpublishing.co.uk

An Empirical View of Business Model Innovation in The Energy Sub-Sector (Electricity) of Nigeria

Abubakar Tanko Mohammed
Department of Economics
Faculty of Management Science
Nile University of Nigeria
babukartanko@gmail.com

Abstract

This study examines Business Model Innovation in energy sub-sector (electricity) of African sub-Saharan region of Nigeria. The research method used is the secondary approach drawn from a synthesis of peer reviewed international and national literature, journal, reports and documents related to business model innovation. Teecee (2010) postulated that the concept of business model lacks theoretical foundation in economics or business studies due to the difference between theoretical and practical approach. In furtherance, analysis and discussion were drawn from empirical review and finding from consulted literature. The major finding of the study revealed that there exists a business model innovation for the energy sub-sector (electricity) in Nigeria, however, the sector is constraint with inadequate financial, human and material capital base, infrastructure, tools for research and development, operational framework and non-robust policies that would provide for the construction of a sustainable business model for the sector. The study recommends that; the government of Nigeria should develop a single policy documents for the various energy sources that will address the issues of dynamism in energy generation, transmission, distribution and pricing; and channel substantial resources to

London International Conferences, 28-30 January 2021, hosted online by UKEY Consulting and Publishing, London, United Kingdom

technological development, research and development in the energy sector; and ensure that only companies that have competence and capacity in the sector are allowed to participate in the process of privatization bidding and award of energy licenses.

Keywords: Business model, innovation, pricing, tariff, energy

1. Introduction

This paper takes a closer look at business model Innovation in the energy sub-sector (electricity) of African Sub-Saharan region of Nigeria, with a view to examine the methodology, concepts and innovation that make up the price mechanism for energy transition. According to USAID (2019) Nigeria is the largest economy in Sub-Sahara Africa, however, limitation in the power sector has continued to constrain growth in the economy. The country has the potential to generate 12,522 megawatts (MW) of electric power from existing plants but is able to generate only about 4,000MW which is inadequate for domestic consumption (USAID, 2019). This brings to question how energy generated is distributed to meet the rising energy demand in the country and what business model is applied for energy transition by the generation, transmission and distribution companies. In furtherance, the major question this paper aim to answer is; how effective/ efficient is the delivery mechanism of the existing business model in energy transitions in Nigeria?

It is a well known fact that Nigeria's major energy source comes from non-renewable (hydro and thermal) power supply solely controlled by the government not until 2005 when the privatization of electricity distribution companies began in (NERC 2005). According to Hannon, Foxon, & Gale's study (as cited in Hall & Roelich, 2016) the dominant supply business model for the electricity has been the corporate utility selling units of energy to consumers in liberalized national market. Could this be the case for the energy sub-sector in Nigeria? To answer this question, the study will examine the various business models used by energy producers in the Nigerian market. In addition, the study aims to contribute to the already existing debate on business model innovation by managers and academics with a view to identify gaps and make recommendations that would serve as a reference point for business managers, academics, government and private organizations. The paper is structured as follows: chapter one (i) deals with the introduction and methodology; chapter two (ii) embodies the main section, which is the theoretical and empirical literature and findings, and chapter three (iii) captures the conclusion and policy recommendations of the paper.

1.1. Research Method

The research method used is a qualitative approach drawn from a synthesis of peer reviewed international and national literature, journal, reports and documents related to business model innovation.

2. Literature Review

2.1. Theoretical Literature

According to Reis (CNBC News 2018), innovation in the energy sector is about decentralization of energy sources and development of business models that satisfy both the producers and consumers of energy in a competing market economy. Globally, innovation is seen to be synonymous with new edge technology and how leading technological companies are been able to change the world around using combinations of various energy sources to development hard ware such as electronic devices and other sophisticated gadgets to programme the way we do things and providing a new level of convenience for household and the business community. Shafer, Smith and Linder's study (as cited in Umihana, 2014) defined business model as representation of a firm's underlying core logic and strategic choices for creating and capturing value within a value network. Foxon's postulated (as cited in Hall & Roelich, 2016) technological and business model innovation must co-evolve with policy and system regulation for energy transitions to be achieved. According Nussey, 2018, innovation is the discovery and development of technologies from different energy sources for onward transmission to the end user, but without a business model that wove all components, innovation cannot be said to be a breakthrough. Nussey, 2018 gave an example of an online transport company Uber and Lyft, have relatively few employees and do not own cars, but even in the face of stringent regulatory resistance that protects existing taxi industry, they were able to develop a business model using new technology to provide a new level of travel convenience through real time online business interaction that taxis didn't offer thereby transforming the transport industry with a more exciting experience for both users and the company. According to Nussey a good business model answers two important questions; how products or services are paid and who is making the profit. Therefore, business models have to be innovative for a product to stand the taste of time.

Two highly respected authors in the field of strategic management and entrepreneurship Amit and Zott's postulated (as cited in Umihana, 2014) that the subject of Business Model Innovation (BMI) is of high significance for managers and academic researchers for three core reasons. First, BMI represents an often underutilized foundation of future value; secondly, producers could find it more difficult to replicate an entire novel activity system than a single novel product, and finally, managers should never undermine the competitor's effort in the BMI area since such innovations are a potentially powerful competitive tool.

In search for the relevant underlying economic theory associated with business model, Teecee's study (as cited in Umihana, 2014) postulated that the concept of business model lacks theoretical foundation in economics or business studies due to the difference between theoretical and practical approach. Teecee argues that the economic theory being a "caricature of the real world" and simply assuming that customers will buy a product if the price is lower than the perceived value, neglects the importance of the concept of business models. On the other side, entrepreneurs and managers have to give a close consideration to the design of business model because "business model are necessary features of market economies where there is customer choice, transaction costs and heterogeneity among consumer and producers, and competition".

Conceptuality, Johnson, Christen and Kagerman' study (as cited in Umihana, 2014) defined four elements that jointly create delivery and capture value in a business model. These are customer value proposition (CVP), profit formula, Key Processes and Key resources. Figure 1below illustrates these factors with their sub-elements.

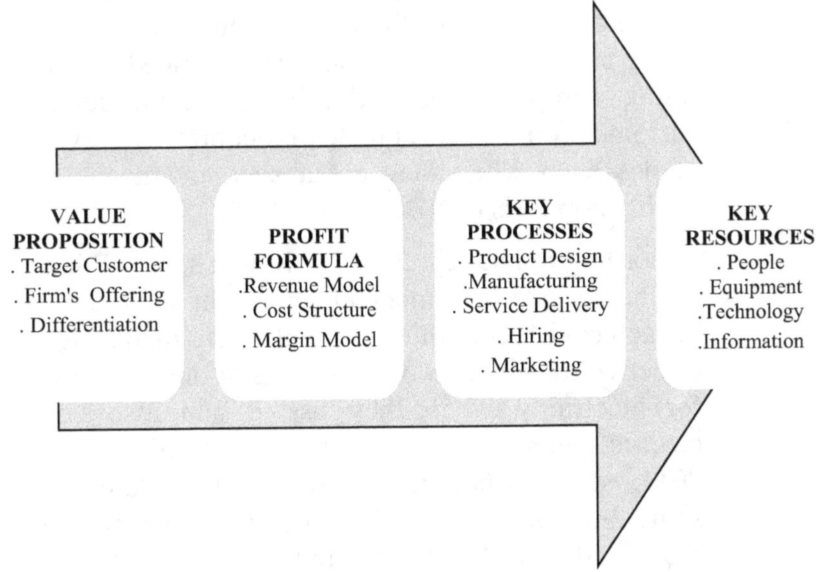

Figure 1 Business Model – Key Components

(adapted from Johnson, Christensen, and Kagermann 2008, p.5)

2.2. Empirical Literature

According to Reis (CNBC News, 2018) who is the Vice President, Head of Innovation B2C E.ON, the company had developed various business models. In the *First business model*; the company sell solar panels and batteries to customers to produce their own energy and with innovation of "Vitual Power Cloud" energy users are able to store energy and use it whenever they want. In the *Second business model*; Energy companies install mega batteries in homes as such customers pay to the energy company instead of the utility company. Lastly, in the *Third business model:* the company had with the aid of mobile devices come up with a solutions for customers that use electric cars, for example, customers receive real time information about the next charging station and its location through application installed on their mobile devices. in addition, digital technology platforms has made it easier for companies to scale customer needs globally, and as a result, companies have developed digital devices that help customers optimize, regulate and control energy usage in their homes even when they are absent, by means of a software application Reis (CNBC News 2018).

According to Nussey, 2018, in 1880 Thomas Edison invented a business model that made electric light affordable to everyone, he achieved economies of scale that made electricity cost–effective for hundred of customers at once. Customers just pay for electricity when they use it and also commercialized electric meter to precise measure and bill usage. In 2010 and 2011, solar installation in the United States experienced a spurt, this was largely due to the development of a business model called Solar Power Purchase Agreements (solar PPA's) which was popularized by pioneer solar company, SunEdison and its CEO, Jigar Shah. They created a simplified, standard approach that let solar buyers avoid upfront capital costs and just pay for the solar power as they used. The business model took away initial technical and financial cost for customers which made the model attractive and acceptable to both producers and consumers (Nussey, 2018).

According to Brookings, 2019, despite the differences in geographic and sector focus of businesses in Africa, what entrepreneurs have in common is the imagination to see the continent unmet needs as opportunities for entrepreneurship and the long term commitment required to build business of meaningful scale. Successful African innovators are also deeply conscious of the barriers to their businesses success, and careful to build long term resilience into their business models. For example, Nigerian based entrepreneur and founder Aliko Dangote, Africa's richest man has build a shock-proof manufacturing model through vertical integration of supply chain, on-site power generation, robust engagement with government and an internal manufacturing academy. This shows that the energy sector can be properly harnessed and sustained if serious investors swing in with the appropriate business model.

2.3. An outlook of International Intervention in Nigeria Electrification Project as Business Model for Electricity Expansion.

Several international organizations have identified the energy sector in Nigeria as a source for global economic expansion. According to World Bank, 2019 under the World Bank Nigeria Electrification Project; the development objective is to increase access to electricity service for households, public educational institution, and underserved Micro, Small, and Medium Enterprise (MSMEs) with an investment of about $756,000 million. The project comprises of four innovative components and business models for its sustainability among which are (i) minimum subsidy tender for mini grids (ii) performance-based grants program (stand-alone solar systems for one million homes and MSMEe at lower cost) (iii) energizing education objective to provide reliable, affordable, and sustainable power to public universities and associated teaching hospitals; and (iv) providing technical assistance to build a framework for rural electrification up-scalling, support project implementation as well as broad capacity building in Rural Electrification Agency (REA), Nigerian Electricity Regulatory Commission (NERC), and other relevant stake holders (World Bank, 2019).

To further support the Nigerian Electrification Project, according to USAID 2019, Power Africa assisted the government of Nigeria with agreements to move the Qua Iboe gas project. This was contained in a World Bank project information document which showed the Bank's board approval of US$395 million for the Azura Edo IPP (Azura) and the Exxon Qua Iboe Independent Power Project (QIPP), (World Bank 2014) and also with agreements on several solar projects that will help diversify the country's energy mix. In addition, interventions such as; a. Transaction advisory; b. Loss reduction work with utilities; and Partnership with National Association of Regulatory Utility Commissioners was rendered.

Power Africa through USAID and the U.S. Trade and Development Agency (USTDA) has collaborated with Nigeria to improve commercial operations and reduce losses at five distribution companies in Nigeria. Power Africa is also supporting off-grid options as well. Through a 15 million Dollars Overseas Private Investment Corporation (OPIC) loan, Lumos Incorporation, is deploying rooftop solar panel kits to approximately 70,000 residential and small commercial customers in Nigeria, using a lease to-own business model. The U.S African Development Foundation (USADF) in partnership with General Electric and other supporting partners in collaboration with Power Africa has awarded $900,000 grants to entrepreneurs for innovative, off-grid energy projects in Nigeria (USAID 2019).

These facts are supported by a World Bank date demonstrated in a graphical presentation in figure 1 below, the graph show that energy supply shortfall in Nigeria are further marred with generally inefficient technical and commercial management of the grid system, leading to interruptions and poor service delivery.

"Power Africa is comprised of 21 U.S Government Agencies, over 145 private companies and 18 bilateral and multilateral development partners to support sub-saharan governments by working together to increase the number of people with access to power. Power Africa's goal is to achieve 30,000MW of new generated power and 60 million new connections by 2030 to reach 300 million Africans. (USAID 2019)"

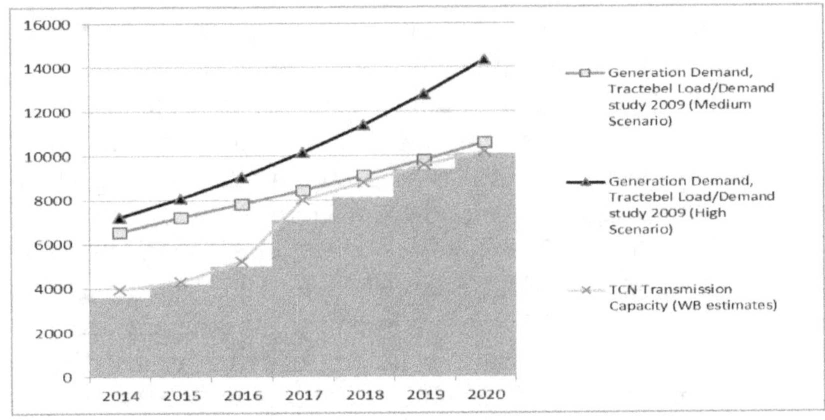

Figure 2: Supply Short Fall in Nigeria

Source: World Bank, 2019.

In 2013, the Mobile for Development Utilities Programme facilitated a joint venture between a mobile and energy company, Mobile Telecommunication Networks (MTN) and a Netherland energy solution company LUMOS launched a solar energy business model innovation that provide consumers energy with power off-grid. The business model innovation is a breakthrough in Nigeria which combines technology from telecommunication and off-grid solar system. The business model provides modern electricity through reliable smart solar systems. The MTN-Lomus Product is made available to buyers

London International Conferences, 28-30 January 2021, hosted online by UKEY Consulting and Publishing, London, United Kingdom

on a lease to own basis and its cost is spread over a year term, payable in affordable instalments via mobile phone from an MTN airtime account. The MTN and LUMOS business model allows a customer to full ownership of the energy system after a total payment within an agreed duration. Lumos produced an 80W pay-as-you-go (PAYG) solar home systems and reached its 500 system goal for the pilot in May 2015 and sold more than 3000 SHS in September 2015.

2.4. Nigeria Energy Sector and Regulations

Public electricity generation in Nigeria began the year 1896, with the installation of 30kw generating set at Marina Lagos by the colonial public works department. In 1950, the Electricity Corporation of Nigerian was established by the legislative council as a central body to integrate electricity supply and development (Sambo, 2008,). By 1969, ECN operated 132 kilovolts at a time when the Niger Dam Authority (NDA) established in 1962 operated 330kilovolts. ECN and NDA were merged by government decree No. 24 of 1972 to create what was then called National Electric Power Authority (NEPA). That decree gave NEPA the mandate to "maintain and coordinate an efficient and economic system of electricity supply for all parts of the federation". The inability of government to effectively manage NEPA called for a new reform of the power sector after the country transited power to a civilian regime in 1999. The reform of the power sector in with the enactment of the Electric Power Sector Reform (EPSR) ACT 2005 opened doors of opportunity for investment by the private sector. Subsequently, the Power Holding Company of Nigeria (PHCN) was formed as a transitional corporation that comprises of eighteen (18) successor companies (Six (6) generation companies, eleven (11) distribution companies and one (1) transmission company) created from NEPA. In 2010, the Nigerian Bulk Electricity Trading Plc (NBET) was establishment as a credible off-taker of electricity power from generation companies. By 2013, the privatization of all generation and ten (10) distribution companies was completed while the privatization of the 11th distribution company was completed in November 2014 with the Federal Government retaining the ownership of the transmission company. (NERC, 2019).

According to USAID (2019) Power Africa has provided support to the Nigerian Electricity Regulatory Commission (NERC) through a partnership with the National Association of Regulatory Utility Commissioners (NARUC). NARUC provides guidance on regulatory practices and tariff settings. According to Nigerian Electricity Regulatory Commission (NERC) 2019 Nigeria has an abundance of renewable energy resources, with a vast and mostly untapped potential in renewable energy sources, NERC has set a target of generating a minimum of 2,000MW of electricity from renewable energy by the year 2020; an assured investors of guaranteed price and access to grid, feed-in-tariff for solar, wind, biomass and small hydro power purchase agreement (PPA) based on plant life circle of 20 years. With a plan for electricity distribution companies (DisCos) to procure 1000MegaWatt (MW) (50%) and Nigerian Bulk Electricity Trading Company (NBET) to procure minimum of 1000MW(50% of the total projected renewable sourced electricity). In line with the National Policy on Renewable Energy and Energy Efficiency, the Commission approved three windows for grid connected renewable energy projects which are:

a) Net-metering for very small capacities (typically below 1MW).

b) Feed-in-tariff for capacities up to; a. 5MW; b. 10MW; c.10MW of Biomass and d. 30MW of small hydro.
c) Competitive tender for capacities above the threshold outlined in "b" to be procured through NBET.
These indicates the willingness of the Nigerian government to open doors of opportunity to the business world to come and invest in a business seen to be very viable and filled with

untapped potential for the growth and development of the energy sector, green revolution and energy market in general (NERC 2019). No doubt, the Nigerian renewable energy market has begun to experience exploration with investment by national and multi-national companies who believe in the future and sustainability of renewable energy. According to United State Energy Information Administration (EIA, 2016), Nigeria's power sector suffers from poor maintenance of electricity facilities, natural gas supply shortages, and inadequate transmission and distribution network. Nigeria has an average daily generation of 4000MW against the actual electricity demand which is placed at an estimated 10,000MW. Nigeria also has one of the lowest rates of net electricity generation per capita in the world (EIA 2016). To support this claim, the USAID Nigeria Power Africa Fact Sheet 2019 stated that Nigeria's current access to electricity supply is at 45%, rural access 30% and Urban 55% respectively while households without power rest at 20million.

This implies that Nigeria has Electricity energy gap of over 6,000,0MW, this identified gap could be seen as an opportunity for entrepreneurs to invest in various sources of energy generation, transmission and distribution in Nigerian. Notwithstanding, out of an average 4000MW daily generation, transmission and distribution still remains a challenge due to poor investment and lack of adequate infrastructure. Licensed Electricity Distribution Companies (Discos) still battle with issue of meter installation, procurement, and distribution and non-payment of energy consumed by some members of the public. All this could be associated with the companies low capital investment in human capital and material resources, weak research and development unit resulting in a weak business model.

2.5. Tariff

According to USAID Nigeria Power Africa Fact Sheet (2019) Nigeria has privatized its electricity distribution companies creating a wide range of tariffs among the distribution companies. Section 32 (d) of the Electric Power Sector Reform (EPRS) Act, 2005 is to ensure that the prices charged by licenses are not only fair to customers but sufficient to allow the licenses to finance their activities and make profit for efficient operation (NERC 2005). It is in view of the EPRS Act that the NERC under Section 76 of the EPSR Act 2005, established a methodology for determining electricity Tariff Order called the Multi-Year Tariff Order (MYTO) model which sets out tariffs for the generation, transmission and distribution of electricity in Nigeria. The MYTO is used to set wholesale and retail prices for electricity in the industry by employing a unified way to determine total industry revenue requirement that is tied to measurable performance improvement and standards. The tariff model is also designed as an incentive based regulation that seeks to reward performance above given benchmarks, reduce technical and non-technical//commercial loses and leads to cost recovery and improved performance standards from all industry operators in the Nigerian Electricity Supply Industry (NESI). The objectives of the MYTO are: (i). cost recovery/financial viability; (ii). certainty and stability framework; (iii). incentive for improving performance; (iv). allocation of risk; and (v). simplicity and cost-effectiveness.

According to Abuja Electricity Distribution Plc Annual Report 2015, in 2008 NERC introduced a Multi-Year Tariff Order (MYTO) as the frame work for determining the industry pricing structure and this forms the basis of revenue earned by the Company after taking into consideration changes as applicable per the Transitional Electricity Market (TEM) rules as issued by NERC. Consequently, the introduction of the MYTO has increased the company revenue by 30% as a result of the 33.20% increase in tariff by NERC from 2014. However, this policy could be said to only be applicable to the non-renewable (hydro) energy sector.

2.6. NERC MYTO Tariff Business Model

The MYTO methodology uses a building blocks approach in setting transmission and distribution tariffs, providing the benefits of both price cap and incentive based regulation. Figure 3 below shows an illustration of the MYTO generation, transmission and distribution business model of the Nigerian Electricity Regulatory Commission (NERC).

NERC MYTO Transmission and Distribution Business Model

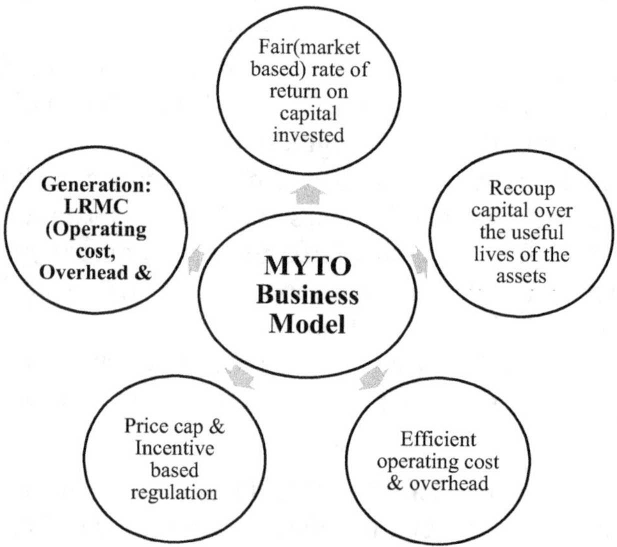

Figure 3: Diagram of NERC MYTO Generation, Transmission and Distribution Business Model

Source: Author

The three building blocks are:

a. The allowed return on capital: Fair (market based) rate of return on capital invested.

b. The allowed return on capital: Recoup capital over the useful lives of the assets (depreciation).
c. Efficient operating costs and overheads.

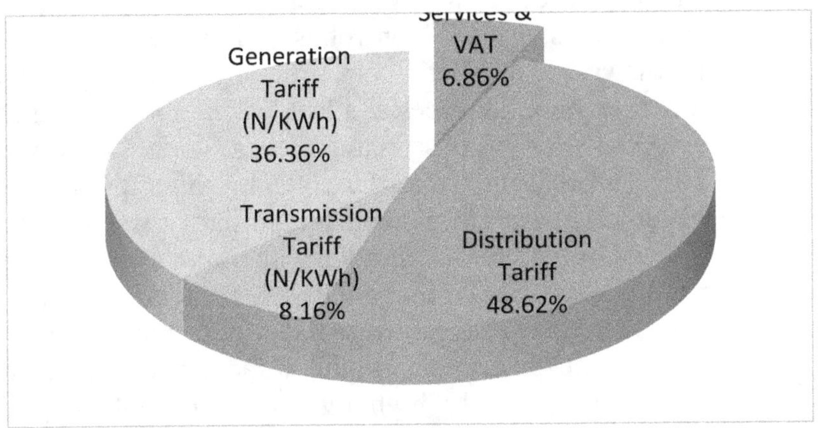

Figure 4: Electricity Tariff share percentage among Generation, Transmission and Distribution companies
(adapted from NERC, 2019)

Generation tariff is determined using a benchmark Long Run Marginal Cost (LRMC) of the most economically efficient new entrant. This offers a transparent framework for determining electricity tariff that engender legitimacy and acceptance by providing for clear dis-aggregation and determination of necessary operating cost and overheads and reasonable Return on Investment. As seen in figure 4 above, out 100% tariff charge by energy companies, distribution companies part with 48.63% being the largest share while generation and transmission companies take 36.36% and 8.16% respectively. The remaining 6.86% serves as services & VAT.

2.7. Challenges of Business Model in Nigeria's Energy Sector

After a critical review of literature, the study categorizes the challenges of business model in Nigeria into three main components; (i) Non-robust Policy and Operational Framework (ii) Deficit in Infrastructure requirements (iii) Macro-economic forces and lack of credit utilities. The categorization of these challenges is supported by World Bank 2019 which stated that the solar in Nigeria lags the regional benchmarks due to general unfamiliarity with the technology and commercial structures, comparable commissioning performance, and power delivery benchmarks and that the price-delivery mechanisms have not been fully developed which contribute to inability to attract private capital at optimal rates and generally high over cost. USAID Nigeria Power Africa Fact Sheet, (2019) also identified some major challenges confronting investment and enabling environment in Nigeria energy sector as; Macroeconomic forces, Lack of creditworthy utilities and Lack of strong and transparent regulator needed to scale up the level of energy poverty in Nigeria.

Also, the MYTO business model developed by the NERC in collaboration with its relevant stake holders in the non-renewal energy sector has failed to meet up with expectations of electricity consumers generally due to lack of capacity of most electricity distribution companies to meet expected energy demand within the MYTO model. Despite the considerable increment in electricity tariff by the NERC, the distribution companies have not been able to meet up expectation. According to an online news report agency the Cable, Awojulugbe 2019, reported that the Government of Nigeria has set up a committee that will review the ownership of the electricity distribution companies (Discos) with intention to invest $250 million to boost the sector. Adding that, the government has spent over N1.7 trillion in the years 2017,

2018 and 2019 which is not sustainable for the government. If this decision comes into effect, then new investors will emerge and the MYTO business model may no longer stand the taste of time in the energy market and would have to give way for a more acceptable business model in a competing market as that of Nigeria.

2.8. Analysis, Discussion and Conclusion

Based on findings from empirical reviews, it is evident that there exist business models in the energy sector of Nigeria for both renewable and non-renewable energy. The introduction of the Multi-Year Tariff Order (MYTO) by NERC in 2005 as the frame work for determining the industry pricing structure which formed the basis for revenue earned by the Distribution Companies after taking into consideration changes as applicable per the Transitional Electricity Market (TEM) rules clearly defines the business model used by the electricity, transmission and distribution companies in Nigeria. The MYTO business model framework also determine the tariff for power generation using the Long Run Marginal Cost (LRMC) calculation to cover for operation cost, overheads and return on investment. However, the application of the MYTO model in the business environment as the sole concept for tariff setting has been challenged by many users. The model is widely criticized and seen as inefficient due the inability of energy producers to deliver quality service to consumers and address complaint that would aid improve the system work in a more efficient manner. The application of the MYTO is yet to test as a preferred and workable model largely because a huge number of household especially in rural areas are yet to be metered. There are also cases of price/unit disparity for different metering system across the distribution companies. This also points to the fact that the distribution companies have not adequately invested as agreed with the NERC on the required level of infrastructure to be put in place within the short-run. Consequently, the energy sector has continued to experience energy wastage and leakages as a result of poor investment in research, expansion of infrastructural base and non-rubost policy and operational framework which form the key components in business model innovation. It is quite clear that financial and human capital is lacking in the overall energy chain in Nigeria.

3. Policy Recommendations

In view of the findings and discussion, the study recommends that the Government of Nigeria;

(a)   Should review and/or develop new policy documents that meet international standards providing price-delivery mechanism that will enable investors develop business models (inclusive of price cap and incentive based regulation) for both renewable and non-renewable energy.

(b)   Develop a single policy documents for the various energy sources that will address the issues of dynamism in energy generation, transmission and distribution and pricing. And possibly look at policies that would encourage energy mix.

(c)   Should channel substantial resources to technological development, research and development in the energy sector and ensure that only companies that have competence and capacity in the sector are allowed to participate in the process of privatization bidding and award of energy licenses.

(d)   Strengthen the capacity of Nigerian Electricity Regulatory Commission by collaboration with sister international agencies on the provision of favourable policy documents and other required mandate to suite the Nigeria's energy business climate.

References

ABC News in-depth (April 4, 2019) Why Australia's booming renewable energy industry has started hitting hurdles [Video file] retrieved on 4/22/2019 from https://www.youtube.com/watch?v=674cUf0DT8A

Abuja Electricity Distribution Plc Annual Report 2015. Retrieved on 5/12/2019 from http://www.nerc.gov.ng/index.php/library/industrystatistics/mfi/132-industry-relations.

Awojulugbe, O. (2019, November 21). El-Rufai appointed head of committee to review ownership of disco. The Press. Retrieved on 28/03/2020 from https://www.thecable.ng/just-in-el-rufai-appointed-head-of-committee-to-review-ownership-of-discos.

Brookings, Africa's Untapped Business Potential. Retrieved on 5/12/2019 from https://www.brookings.edu/research/spotlighting opportunities-for-business-in-africa-and-strategies-to-succeed-in-the-worlds-next-big-growth-market/

CNBC International TV (2018, February 23) Energy Sector (B2C) | I.O.T. Powering The Digital Economy: Retrieved on https://www.youtube.com/watch?v=ExMzdN4bfOI&t=680s

Daily energy sent out; Nigerian Electricity Regulatory Commission. Retrieved on 5/2/2019 from https://www.nercng.org/index.php/library/industry-statistics/generation/374-energy-sent#information.

EIA BETA. Retrieved on 05/13/201 from https://www.eia.gov/beta/international/analysis.php?iso=NGA

Hall, S., & Roelich, K. (2016). Business model innovation in electricity supply markets: The role of complex value in the United Kingdom. *Energy Policy*, *92*, 286-298. Retrieved on 3/1/2020 From https://www.sciencedirect.com/science/article/pii/S030142151630060X.

Lumos: Pay-as-you-go solar in Nigeria with MTN – GSMA. Retrieved On 2/27/2021 from https://www.gsma.com/mobilefordevelopment/wp-content/uploads/2016/11/Case-Study-Lumos-Pay-as-you-go-solar-in-Nigeria-with-MTN.pdf

Nigeria Electrification Project. Retrieved on 5/13/2019 from http://projects.worldbank.org/P161885?lang=en.

Nigerian Electricity Regulatory Commission. Retrieved 5/12/2019. https://www.nercng.org/index.php/home/operators.

Nussey, B (2018) Using new business models to unleash competition and innovation in the power industry retrieved on 4/22/2019 from https://www.freeingenergy.com/using-new-business-models-to-unleash-competition-and-innovation-in-the-power-industry/.

Renewable energy sourced electricity. Retrieved on 5/12/2019 from https://www.nercng.org/index.php/home/operators/renewable-energy

Sambo, A. S. (2008). Matching electricity supply with demand in Nigeria. *International Association of Energy Economics*, *4*, 32-36.

Umihana, U (2014) Business model innovation as a new source of competitive advantage: A case study based on the energy sector. Retrieved on 4/24/2019 from https://www.researchgate.net/publication/317672160_Business_Model_Innovation_as_a_New_Source_of_Competitive_Advantage_-_A_Case_Study_based_on_the_Energy_Sector

USAID Nigeria Power Africa Fact Sheet. Retrieved on 5/12/2019 from https://www.usaid.gov/powerafrica/nigeria.

World Bank Project Information Document. Retrieved on 514/2019 from http://documents.worldbank.org/curated/en/680081467998213622/98822-PID-P155000-PUBLIC-Box3931.

londonic.uk   ukeyconsultingpublishing.co.uk

SWOT Analysis of Electronic Publishing: Example of UKEY Publishing

Selim Ozdemir
UKEY Publishing
selim.tx@gmail.com

Mehmet Ali Eroglu
UKEY Publishing
dr@emali.org

Abstract

The emergence and development of electronic publishing will be examined in this study. In particular, analysis of the effects of electronic books and other electronic publications on the publishing sector will be included. What opportunities and threats can be discussed? while examining the strengths and weaknesses of the electronic publishing industry comparatively. It will be examined as a UKEY Publishing case study.

The feedback to be received at the conference will be evaluated and the study will be expanded as an article. The study will include quantitative and qualitative research findings.

Keywords: Electronic publishing, e-book, SWOT, strength, weaknesses, opportunities, threats.

London International Conferences, 28-30 January 2021, hosted online by UKEY Consulting and Publishing, London, United Kingdom

London International Conferences

londonic.uk   ukeyconsultingpublishing.co.uk

Digital Transformation and Business Model

Teymur Valiyev
SOCAR Georgia Gas
t.valiyev@socar.ge

Abstract

The main purpose of this paper is to understand digital transformation process and its main components through comprehensive analysis of existing academic literature. The paper tries to shed light on the definition of digital transformation by summarising opinions of different scholars. The author disassembles digital transformation into components and then assembles them in a new framework for further analysis in the dissertation. Discussion of digital strategy, digital business model, as well as each digital enabler – culture, people, structure and processes, and digital driver – technology, data, customer and innovation aim to elaborate their impact on digital transformation process.

Keywords: digital, transformation, strategy

London International Conferences, 28-30 January 2021, hosted online by UKEY Consulting and Publishing, London, United Kingdom

1. Introduction

Over the last decades, introduction of new information and communication technologies and computerisation of processes have led to fundamental shifts in the ways enterprises work. Increased usage of software applications and mobile devices made digital technologies one of the vital elements of enterprise systems. Things and data started to become digital since the second part of last century. Gartner (2016) explains digitalisation as the adoption of digital technologies in business and society and the associated changes in the connectivity of individuals, organisations, and objects. While digitisation refers to the technical process of converting analogue signals into a digital form, digitalisation refers to using digital technologies in broader individual, organisational, and societal contexts (Legner et al., 2017). In early times digitalisation only concerned IT people, those are software and hardware related employees, but it now affects all business functions, and is embedded into daily routines of enterprises.

Businesses have always changed the way they do things. They changed suppliers when found better options, they changed market position, when renewed their target, they changed business models when current value propositions did not match the demand, and they changed strategies when faced new horizons. When all or most of these changes happened together and in a bigger scale, then business transformation occurred. Introduction of enterprise business applications like Enterprise Resource Planning (ERP) and Customer Relationship Management (CRM), rise of social media (Facebook, twitter, Instagram, etc.), expansion of smartphones and data led to a new wave of business transformation, this time digital transformation. Westerman (2011) states that, at this stage, business transformation is not just digital, transformation cannot do without digital.

London International Conferences, 28-30 January 2021, hosted online by UKEY Consulting and Publishing, London, United Kingdom

In line with increased usage of digital technologies and digital transformation practices, academic journals, business literature and even social pages gave more space and attention to the topic. This has created a complexity around what was a relatively simple concept, and digital transformation became a huge bucket of anything that relates to business and IT (Chan, 2018). In this regard, it would make sense to shed light on the definition of digital transformation.

One of the earliest papers on digital transformation by Andal-Ancion, Cartwright and Yip (2003) discusses the impact of new information technologies (NIT) on business strategy. The authors describe the ways drivers of NIT change traditional value chain and disintermediate value flows. Bonnet and Ferraris (2011) link digital transformation to operational processes and customer service, and defines it as the increasing adoption of digital tools and technologies by an organisation to fundamentally change both its internal and external processes. According to McAffee (2011), digital transformation is characterised by the ever growing penetration of digital technologies into every facet of business life. By digital technologies, he means broad usage of enterprise applications, analytics tools, corporate hardware systems and individual devices. Fitzgerald et al (2013) defines digital transformation as the use of new digital technologies to enable major business improvements, such as enhancing customer experience, streamlining operations or creating new business models. Hemerling et al (2018) brings in the cultural dimension, and states that like any major transformation, a digital transformation requires instilling a culture that supports the change while enabling the company's overarching strategy. Nicholas Carr's (2003) seminal article led to the debates among scholars and business representatives on significance of IT for strategic differentiation. In his view, not the technology itself, but what the company does with it is important.

2. Framing digital transformation

London International Conferences, 28-30 January 2021, hosted online by UKEY Consulting and Publishing, London, United Kingdom

Examination of academic literature revealed three different, to some extent comprehensive frameworks of digital transformation. Their main component described below in Figure 4.1.

#	Name of the framework	Components	Source
1	Navigating digital transformation: A framework	1. Digital strategy & transformation 2. People 2.0 3. Digital customer experience 4. Analytics 5. Digital operations 6. Technology strategy & transformation	Bonnet and Ferraris, 2011: p.23
2	Digitisation requires mastering in six action fields	1. Customer 2. Data 3. Value proposition 4. Organisation 5. Operations 6. Transformation management	Gimpel et al., 2018: p.38
3	Digital congruence	1. Strategy 2. Tasks 3. Culture 4. People 5. Structure	Kane et al., 2016: p.14

Figure 1 – Digital transformation frameworks

The author of this paper tried to construct a new framework by enhancing the model of Kane et al. (2016) with more "hard" and "state-of-the-art" concepts. In this sense, we used core ideas of "the implications for strategy in a smart, connected world" proposed by Porter and Hepperman (2014). According to Porter (2014), firms face ten new strategic choices driven by the characteristics of smart, connected products (Appendix 1: Figure 10.4). We identified four drivers – data, technology, customer and innovation, which are core to Porter's framework and at the same time, very popular in the literature on digital transformation, and called them "transformation drivers". We also added separate business model layer (Figure 4.2). Although business model is included to a wider component of strategy, it is still a significant element of transformation process and therefore, needs to be studied separately.

The framework is constructed in a pyramid form. Vertical allocation of components means that transformation enablers and drivers are integral to business model, which in turn is a part of digital strategy. The horizontal dimension stands for transformation process, during what all components interact with each other and move towards a common goal. The author discusses the following sections of this chapter according to this framework.

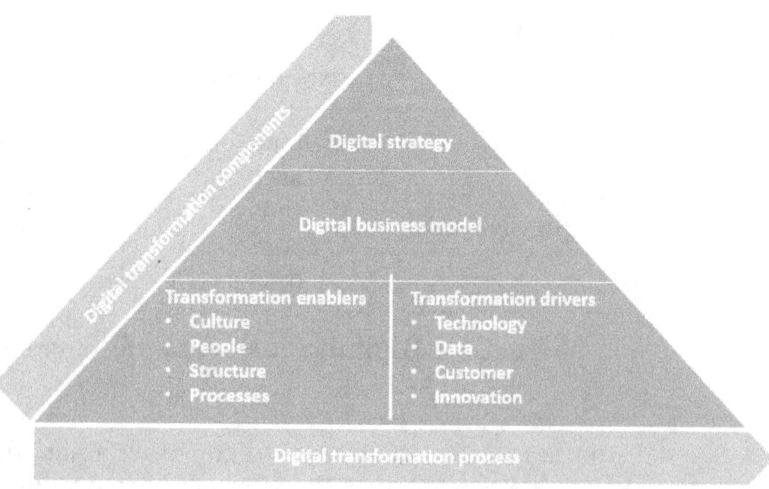

Figure 2 – Digital transformation framework

3. Digital strategy

Adoption of digital strategy is the strongest differentiator between the most successful firms in digital transformation and the rest (Fitzgerald et al, 2013). Companies need to follow a careful step toward digital transformation, designing a winning strategy and a clear roadmap across people, processes, and technology (Bonnet and Ferraris, 2011). Although Westerman (2017) warns not to call this a "digital strategy", the term is widely used in academic literature and business journals. He argues that "creating a digital strategy can focus the organisation in ways that don't capture the true value of digital transformation. You don't need a digital strategy. You need a better strategy, enabled by digital". On the other hand, in essence, the academia agrees with the point of view of Westerman. For instance, Kane et al (2017) assert that digital strategies are not about implementing technologies for the sake of becoming more digital, but they involve the opportunity for greatest business impact. Digital strategy shifts the focus of IT functions from software and IT related operations to agile business innovations that leverage digital technologies (Gimpel et al, 2018).

Digital strategy also cannot be incremental; only inventive strategic plans are going to work (Catlin et al, 2018). While in digital strategies companies take a longer view (Kane et al, 2017), on the execution part, companies should not fall into trap by pushing envelopes too far and too fast (Westerman, 2017). The research conducted by Kane et al (2016) identified that most successful companies in Silicon Valley, to be effective in digital environment, choose ten-to-twenty-year timeframes for their digital strategy. To address the digital future, while meeting today's needs, they use the zoom-out/zoom-in approach. The zoom-out dimension looks at a time horizon of ten or more years by predicting long-term market trends and customer expectations. The zoom-in component is responsible for the next six to twelve months by identifying few business initiatives with the greatest potential to have an impact on the longer-term destination.

These instructions of LIC provide you guidelines for preparing papers for International Conference on social sciences, management, economics, humanities, and interdisciplinary sciences. Use this document as a template and as an instruction set. These instructions of LIC provide you guidelines for preparing papers for International Conference on social sciences, management, economics, humanities, and interdisciplinary sciences. Use this document as a template and as an instruction set.

4. Digital business model

Tremendous success stories of digital giants, like Apple, Google, Amazon and Facebook should not mislead us on the true reasons of business growth. A digital platform, or a digital solution may drive the growth, but the engine of transformation is the business model. According to Johnson, Christensen and Kagermann (2008), a business model consists of four interlocking elements that create and deliver value: customer value proposition, profit formula, key resources and key processes. In short, business model is a simplified representation of how companies do their business. Business Model Canvas, the most popular framework in business literature, allows enterprises to easily describe their infrastructure, offering, customers and finances (Osterwalder and Pigneur, 2010). Iansiti suggests that "a business model is defined by two things: how the organisation creates value for its customers and how it captures that value. Digital transformation changes both" (Iansiti and Lakhani, 2014: p.5).

Software and technology companies have initiated several new, digitally enabled business models. Many enterprise software application vendors, Microsoft, SAP, Oracle among others, are switching from one-time license-selling model to monthly or periodically subscription model, by decreasing capital expenditures (CapEx) and increasing operating expenditures (OpEx) of clients and having more tightened relationship with them (Fitzgerald, 2013). Development of cloud technologies enriched utilisation of this model (Hardy, 2018). Companies now offer their hand on software (Software-as-a-Service, SaaS), development platform (Platform-as-a-Service, PaaS) or server and network infrastructure (Infrastructure-as-a-service, IaaS) as cloud-based monthly services without full purchase and ownership.

The "platform" business model, obviously, currently is one of the widely applied business models (Van Alstyne et al, 2016). Uber, Airbnb, Spotify and many other prominent digital companies, which do not own physical infrastructure and assets employ this business model. Platforms bring together producers and consumers and allow them to share information and interact with each other. "Network effect" is central to this model. While traditional "pipeline" businesses create value by controlling a linear series of activities – the classic value chain, platforms only own and control their platform, where drivers meet with riders, and buyers reach to sellers.

5. Digital transformation enablers

Organisations need to be prepared for digital transformation. The author of this paper will use a new concept to assess the components, which enable or boost digital transformation, named "digital transformation enablers": culture, people, structure and processes. However, enablement is not a natural characteristic of these components, they need to become enablers. Moreover, without proper treatment, they can act as inhibitors of digital transformation.

5.1.   Culture

Although digital strategies and business models of successful companies can vary from one organisation and industry to another, cultural characteristics remain almost the same for all of them (Kane et al, 2016). Creativity, agility, intellectual stimulation and positive peer relations are among the traits of the digital culture.

Aligning the existing corporate culture with new digital realities inhibits the digital transition of companies (Bonnet and Ferraris, 2011). Digitally maturing companies are constantly cultivating their culture with a strong emphasis on innovation and flexibility. Developing a digital culture may require significant shifts in corporate behaviour.

In fact, corporate culture and digital transformation are mutually interdependent phenomena. Leaders need to cultivate the right culture to digital maturity, on the other hand digital capabilities also drive the culture and its traits (Marchand and Peppard, 2013).

Risk-taking, perhaps, is the most important characteristic of innovative companies (King and Lawley, 2016). Companies blend it with rapid experimentation and agility to increase fast learnings and minimise potential damages. People need to perceive that their organisation is willing to take risks, what drives transformational projects in uncertain circumstances. Hemerling (2018) lists following five core characteristics of digital culture: more external, rather than internal orientation (listen to customers, learn customer experience); delegation over control; encouragement of boldness over caution (risk, fail fast and learn); more action and less planning (agility); collaboration over individual efforts (teamwork).

Corporate culture is one of the main factors in retaining senior bright minds and attracting new digital talents (Booth et al, 2018). Millennials are seeking digital companies with their promise of collaborative, creative environment and greater autonomy (Hemerling, 2018).

5.2.   People

Digital transformation and new project management approaches bring in the roles, which were not existing before in corporate structures. Product owners, scrum masters, customer experience designers, DevOps (Development-Operation) specialists are just few of them. Companies are not only struggling to find the right people for right positions, but also trying to adapt their HR practices and procedures in line with the demand of new digital era (Marchand et al, 2013). Emphasising significance of human resources, Bonnet and Ferraris (2011) state that it is not technology that is the obstacle to digital transformation, it is people.

Digital landscape is changing skills of both IT and non-IT related people. Now sales team includes solution architects with advanced analytics capabilities to develop and demonstrate business outcomes (Iansiti, 2014). It is vital to develop a mix of digital competences across all functions, such as marketing, HR, sales, and IT (Bonnet and Ferraris, 2011). Digitally powered tools must embrace the entire employee lifecycle and completely change the way people join, learn, perform, earn, grow and leave the company (Westerman et al, 2011). Companies create online learning platforms to teach their talent.

Some surveys show that soft skills trump technology knowledge in driving digital transformation (Gimpel et al, 2018). In general, companies are looking for people who have a balance of technical and soft skills. The balance becomes especially clear when looking at the STEAM movement, which advocates adding "art" to the traditional STEM stack of science, technology, engineering, and math (Kane et al, 2016). The emerging roles in digital projects as user-interface and user-experience designers require a background in liberal arts, as much as in computer science. In fact, new-era digital specialists also value a reasonable work-life balance and the stability of large, established company (Booth et al, 2018).

5.3. Structure

Organisations can follow many paths to structuring their digital transformation projects. Smart, connected products have a major impact on both differentiation and integration in organisations, which are two basic elements of the structure (Porter and Hepperman, 2015). Many companies work to limit the power of a single individual or department (Fitzgerald, 2013). They prefer horizontal relationship to hierarchical structures. It improves flexibility and transparency at workplace and promotes innovative culture. Meanwhile, lack of clear structures and rules may hinder transformation efforts.

Porter and Hepperman (2015), as a result of recent digital trends, highlight the organisation of three new functional units. Due to the growing volume, complexity, and strategic importance of data, as many as a quarter of all large firms have dedicated data units, responsible for unified data management and driving the application of advanced data analytics. Another functional group, the dev-ops, is responsible for managing and optimising the ongoing performance of digital products. It brings together IT, software and network specialists (the "dev") and the operational team members (the "ops"). A third new unit, usually called customer experience management, is responsible for managing the customer experience and ensuring that customers get the most from the product.

5.4. Processes

Simplification and automation of business processes is a primary output of digitalisation. In order to automate processes, organisations need to describe and optimise them. This is not as simple task as it sounds. Not surprisingly, many enterprise software application implementation projects fail due to unpreparedness of business processes (Kane et al, 2016).

Digitalisation requires an integrated, flexible IT infrastructure and digital operations, supply networks, and manufacturing capabilities (Iansiti and Lakhani, 2014). A critical challenge of digital manufacturing is the integration of information technologies and operational technologies (IT-OT), which relies on close integration of business related information systems (e.g., ERP, CRM) and operations-related information systems, like manufacturing execution systems (Gimpel et al, 2018). Mobile technologies allowed to digitally document and control field service operations. Porter and Heppelman (2015) insist that we are seeing a whole new era of lean production management. Thanks to the data collected from smart, connected products, waste will be eliminated, sensors in a real-time mode will define production downtimes, and analytics system will predict maintenance schedules. Digital manufacturing enables organisations to enhance manufacturing quality and efficiency via digital end-to-end processes, ranging from design and engineering, production and shipping, to use and refurbishment (Gimpel et al, 2018). Besides core operations, digital technologies change corporate support functions or administrative processes, too. Many company officials confirm that digitalisation sharply improved their internal communications, especially through using social media (Fitzgerald et al, 2013).

6. Digital transformation drivers

Digital transformation drivers – digital technology, data, digital customer behaviours and product and service innovation – stand for the external forces interacting with and amplified by a set of factors originated from organisation's internal environment. Virtually, these are proxies of trends and successful benchmarks derived from the global digital transformation practices.

The drivers do not always act as a standalone component. In contrary, in most cases they appear as a complex of drivers, that are difficult to separate. Leadership needs to make strategic choices on what drivers or set of drivers to follow.

6.1.   Technology

Digital technologies go beyond the classic term of information technologies, which merely associated with computer systems. Digital technology has three fundamental properties different from analogue ones (Iansiti, 2014): unlike analogue signals, digital signals can be transmitted perfectly, without error. Digital signals can be replicated simultaneously indefinite times, and third, ready digital content can be communicated to the incremental consumer at almost zero marginal cost.

Nowadays, main digital transformation technologies include the four groups commonly abbreviated as SMAC: social, mobile, analytics, and cloud (Gimpel et al, 2018). While these technologies are already in widespread use, new technological trends include the Internet of things (IoT), artificial intelligence, blockchain, 3D/4D printing, wearables and augmented and virtual reality. Research conducted by Kane et al (2017) showed that, while led by analytics, SCAM technologies are still important for organisations, in near future, IoT and cognitive technologies will increase their significance.

Technology typically is not simply an add-on to existing processes and practices. Instead, it prompts the companies to rethink how they do business. Digital technology spurs collaboration and helps overcome the common barriers of functional silos (Kane et al, 2017). While technologies drive business transformation process, legacy technology may become obstacle Fitzgerald et al, 2013). Existing systems can be complex to update, especially when integrating to new kinds of technology. The companies need to establish two-speed IT architecture for successful transformation (Booth et al, 2016). Both environments of existing IT architecture, and flexible test-oriented infrastructure should work in line with transformational goals.

6.2.   Data

This is a common belief that data and analytics is the foundation of success in a digital economy. P. Sondergaard from Gartner Research supplemented "data is the new oil" mantra with an original phrase – "analytics is the combustion engine" (Gimpel et al, 2018).

New data sources such as digital transactions, social media usage, embedded sensors, and mobile devices drive data explosion. Corporations go through digital transformation in order "to become more scientific in their decision-making, to rely less on gut feelings and be more data-driven" (McAfee, 2011:31). He states that analytics tools provide companies with a capability to test their initial hypotheses with near-scientific validity.

Davenport (2013) argues that the use of data is as old as decision making itself, but the field of business analytics was born in the mid-1950s. The author differs three eras in the use of analytics. In the era of business intelligence, what he calls Analytics 1.0, new computing technologies and business intelligence software were key in capturing information and reporting it. Since mid-2000s, during the era of big data (Analytics 2.0), internet-based and social network companies started to amass and analyse new kinds of data. Finally,

Analytics 3.0 is the era of data-enriched offerings, where data smartness embedded into the products and services customers buy (Davenport, 2013). Porter and Hepperman (2015), supports the idea that smart, connected products supplies the traditional and mainly internal sources of data with a new source – the product itself. Smart devices can generate real-time readings that are unprecedented in their variety and volume. Data now stands on par with people, technology, and capital as a core asset of enterprises.

Davenport (2006) calls companies advanced in data as analytics competitors, which go well beyond basic statistics by using predictive modelling and sophisticated quantitative techniques. Analytics competitors manage centralised groups to ensure that critical data and other resources are well managed and different units can share data easily, in a structured and consistent formats. Marchand and Peppard (2013) emphasise that traditional IT projects, which focus on technology deployment and analytics projects, which aimed at data exploration should be governed differently. It is crucial to understand how people create and use information, attract cognitive behavioural scientists and take iterative experiments in order to succeed in big data and analytics projects.

6.3.   Customer

An actor, who gained significant power in digital era is the customer. Customers are increasingly becoming better informed and distrusting of traditional marketing methods and instead are turning to online social networks, community forums, blogs and vlogs. The creative ones monetise their knowledge and experience by influencing others on social pages. Today, consumers trust consumers more than they trust brands (Bonnet and Ferraris, 2011). The high adoption rate of mobile devices and tablets, as well as social media and collaboration applications is changing the way people share information, learn, communicate, and interact (Fitzgerald, 2013).

Digital leaders choose a strict customer-first strategy. This is not only about assigning to customer service the highest priority, but continuously following customer behaviours in order to get more insights. Organisations with an up-to-date digital agenda benefits from a greater understanding of how digital technologies, which can seamlessly immerse into customers' lives, affect customer experience at every single touch point (Gimpel et al, 2018). Data gathered based on customer experience, provides companies with insights into their customers' mind-sets, moods, motivations, desires, and aspirations. These insights lead to the development of new products and services, design of new digital customer journeys, and consequently, improvement of customer satisfaction (Grebe et al, 2018).

Enhanced with modern analytical tools, companies can obtain competitive advantage through extracting better customer insights, maximising customer lifetime value, improving retention, up-selling and cross-selling new products (Marchand and Peppard, 2013). Companies need to define which activities they can perform better than customers, and conversely, what activities customers can perform better than the enterprise.

6.4.   Innovation

As a driver of digital transformation, innovation stands for the new, feasible products and services, as well as business practices employed in transformation process. We agree that in some cases, digital technology and digital innovation can be used as interchangeable terms. However, innovation, even a digital one, is a deeper notion, which must possess originality and usability characteristics (Davila et al, 2012). Digital innovation embraces also practices around particular technology, or processes related to it. For instance, discussing investments in digital innovations, Kane et al (2016) mention that in some companies, most important innovations are their funding models. It is critical for an innovative solution to become self-financing, which makes this sustainable.

Product and service innovations can fundamentally reshape the industries. Porter and Hepperman (2014) state that the innovative nature of smart, connected products can expand the very definition of the industry itself. The competitive boundaries of an industry widen to encompass a set of related innovative products that together meet a broader underlying need.

At some points, participants of digital transformation process may become fatigue of the degree of innovation, and ask to take a break (Fitzgerald et al, 2013). However, once you start, innovation never stops. Companies have to develop a continuous process for digital innovation.

7. Results

Digital transformation is comparatively new concept, as the earliest article cited by the author on the topic is dated to 2003. However, during this limited period of time academic literature has granted enough space to the discussion of digitalisation and related theories. Extensive examination of academic journals and management papers revealed that digital transformation touches several components of business life, which were systemised by the author in a new digital transformation framework. Main conclusions of the paper can be summarised as following:

- Companies need to have a long-term digital strategy, which is integrated to overall business strategy, and supported on senior level.
- Digital economy changes the ways of doing business and digitally maturing companies reinvent their business models to meet new challenges and opportunities. In order

to succeed against digital disruptors, incumbent companies can reshape their value capturing models with the help of digital technologies.

- Digital enablers – culture, people, structure and processes have enormous potential to boost digital transformation process, however, without relevant treatment they will inhibit the process.
- Successful companies invest in digital technology, data, customer experience and innovations to drive their business transformation.

London International Conferences, 28-30 January 2021, hosted online by UKEY Consulting and Publishing, London, United Kingdom

References

Andal-Ancion A., Cartwright P., and Yip G. (2003). The digital transformation of traditional businesses, MIT Sloan Management Review, 44(4), 34-41

Bonnet, D. and Ferraris, P. (2011). *Transform to the Power of Digital: Digital Transformation as a Driver of Corporate Performance,* Digital Transformation Review, 01, pp. 14-29

Booth, A., de Jong, E. and Peters, P. (2018). *Accelerating digital transformations: a playbook for utilities,* McKinsey Digital, January, 2018.

Booth, A., Mohr, N. and Peters, P. (2016). *The digital utility: new opportunities and challenges.* McKinsey & Company, Electric power and natural gas, May, 2016.

Catlin T., LaBerge L. and Varney S. (2018). *Digital strategy: the four fights you have to win,* McKinsey Quarterly, October 2018

Carr N.G., (2003). *IT doesn't matter,* Harvard Business Review, 81, pp. 41-49

Christensen, C.; Raynor, M, and McDonald, R. (2015). *What is Disruptive Innovation,* Harvard Business Review, December, pp. 44-53

Davenport, T.H. (2006). *Competing on analytics.* Harvard Business Review, 84, pp.98-107

Davenport, T.H. (2013). *Analytics 3.0.* Harvard Business Review, December, 2013

Davila, T., Epstein, M.J. and Shelton, R. (2012), *Making Innovation Work - How to Manage it, Measure it and Profit from it* (Updated edition). Upper Saddle River, N.J.: FT Press

Fitzgerald M., Kruschwitz N., Bonnet D., Welch M. (2013). *Embracing Digital Technology: A New Strategic*

London International Conferences, 28-30 January 2021, hosted online by UKEY Consulting and Publishing, London, United Kingdom

Imperative. MIT Sloan Management Review, Research Report

Gartner (2016). *IT glossary – digitalization.* [online], Available from: http://www.gartner.com/itglossary/digitalization/ (Accessed on 07.01.2020)

Gimpel H., Hosseini S., Huber R., Probst L., Roeglinger M., Faisst, U. (2018). *Structuring digital transformation: A framework of action fields and its application at Zeiss.* Journal of Information Technology Theory and Application, 19 (1), pp. 31-54

Grebe, M., Ruesmann, M., Leyh, M. and Franke, M.R. (2018). Digital maturity is paying off. Boston Consulting Group

Hemerling, J.; Kilmann, J.; Danoesastro, M.; Stutts, L. and Ahern, C. (2018). *It's Not a Digital Transformation Without a Digital Culture.* [online], Available from: https://www.bcg.com/publications/2018/not-digital-transformation-without-digital-culture.aspx (Accessed on 07.01.2020)

Iansiti M. and Lakhani K.R. (2014). *Digital ubiquity: How connections, sensors, and data are revolutionizing business.* Harvard Business Review, November, 2014.

Kane G.C., Palmer D., Philips A.N., Kiron D. and Buckley N. (2016). *Aligning the Organization for Its Digital Future.* MIT Sloan Management Review and Deloitte University Press

Kane G.C., Palmer D., Philips A.N., Kiron D. and Buckley N. (2017). *Achieving digital maturity. Adapting your company to a changing world.* MIT Sloan Management Review and Deloitte University Press

King, D. and Lawley, S. (2016). *Organisational Behaviour.* Oxford: Oxford University Press

Legner, C., Eymann, T., Hess, T., Matt, C., Böhmann, T., Drews, P., Mädche, A., Urbach, N. and Ahlemann, F. (2017). *Digitalization: Opportunity and challenge for the business and information systems engineering community.* Business & Information Systems Engineering, 59(4), 301-308.

Marcand, D.A. and Peppard, J. (2013). *Why IT fumbles analytics.* Harvard Business Review, January-February, 2013.

McAfee, A. (2011). *I can't think of any industry sector or company which is immune from digital transformation* Digital Transformation Review, 01, pp. 30-35

Osterwalder, A. and Pigneur, Y. (2010). *Business Model Generation: A Handbook for Visionaries, Game Changers, and Challengers.* New York: John Wiley & Co.

Porter, M. and Heppelmann, J. (2014). *How smart, connected products are transforming competition.* Harvard Business Review, 92(11), 64-88

Porter, M. and Heppelmann, J. (2015). *How smart, connected products are transforming companies.* Harvard Business Review, 93(10), 96-114

Van Alstyne, M.W., Parker G.G and Choudary S.P. (2016). Pipelines, platforms and the new rules of strategy. Harvard Business Review, April 2016

Westerman, G., McAfee, A., Bonnet, D., Calmejane, C., Ferraris. P. (2011). *Digital transformation: A roadmap for billion-dollar organizations.* MIT Center for Digital Business and Capgemini Consulting, p. 1-68

Westerman, G. (2017). *Your company doesn't need a digital strategy.* MIT Sloan Management Review, Strategy

London International Conferences

londonic.uk   ukeyconsultingpublishing.co.uk

Attitude of The Top Scorers Towards Societal Cancer

R. Malini
PG Department of Commerce and Research Centre,
Sri Parasakthi College for Women, Courtallam
maliniramu@yahoo.co.in

R. Raghadevi
PG Department of Commerce and Research Centre,
Sri Parasakthi College for Women, Courtallam
ragachandran@gmail.com

Abstract

The social and economic participation of human beings are inevitable to develop their skills for the sustainable development in the society. The organized and unorganized crimes are the root cause for societal cancer and education is the medicine for this ailment. Hence, the society expects higher contribution from top scorers of the higher educational institutions to heal the societal cancer. With this back drop, the attitude of the top scorers towards societal cancer has been studied with the help of primary data collected from 305 top rank holders of Tamil Nadu State Government Universities through questionnaire by adopting cluster sampling technique. Percentage analysis, and Sign test has been applied to analyse the collected data. The result revealed that 95 percent of the respondents expressed their attitude against hunger, poverty, child /women harassment, water wastage and poor sanitation.

London International Conferences, 28-30 January 2021, hosted online by UKEY Consulting and Publishing, London, United Kingdom

But, only 3/4th of the respondents' attitude against corruption, destruction of natural resources and unhealthy food habits is not enough to attain the sustainable development in the society. Therefore, educated people should take part in politics and unite together utmost against societal cancer.

Keywords: Societal Cancer, Education, Top Scorers

1. Introduction

Be the change that you wish to see in the world – Mahatma Gandhi

Humans can't able to live alone because man is a social animal and they depend on each other to fulfill their needs and wants. Hence, social and economic participation are inevitable to develop their skills for the sustainable development in the society. The organized crimes like terrorism, corruption, religious disharmony and drugs and alcohol have interlinked among many rebel groups bring illegal money deposit negative impact on economic development of the society. Unorganized crimes like, child labor, child marriage, child/women harassment, hunger and poverty destroy mental and physical well-being of human being, withdraw their education and interrupt their social participation. Hence, the organized and unorganized crimes are the source for societal cancer to attain the healthy and sustainable development in the society.

Hunger is the root of the societal cancer and it forces the human beings to go down the erroneous pathway to feed themselves and their family. The natural resources are destructed for the well-being and living of present without considering the future generation for their survival in this society. Education is the key to eradicate poverty, prevent societal cancer. Life Skills obtained through education enables the young people to make a positive contribution by understanding their rights and responsibilities. The society will expect higher contribution from top scorers produced by higher educational institutes towards societal wellbeing for the sustainable development. The attitude of the top scores against societal cancer to be determined by the way they think, feel and behave. With this hope, the scope of present research work is determined to scrutinize the attitude of the top scorers towards societal cancer.

London International Conferences, 28-30 January 2021, hosted online by UKEY Consulting and Publishing, London, United Kingdom

Objectives of the study

- To assess the attitude of the top scorers towards societal cancer.
- To analyze whether there is any significant difference in the attitude of the top scorers towards societal cancer.
- To offer suitable suggestions to improve the top scorers' attitude against societal cancer.

Hypothesis of the study

H_0: There is no significant difference in the attitude of the top scorers towards societal cancer.

H_1: There is a significant difference in the attitude of the top scorers towards societal cancer.

2. Research methodology

Source: Both primary and secondary data were used for the study. The primary data were collected through the structured questionnaire sent via e-mail, mail and over the phone. The secondary data were collected from the Controller of Examinations of Tamil Nadu State Government Universities.

Sampling Technique: The primary data were collected by adopting cluster sampling technique.

Sample Size: The sample respondents consist of 305 Top Rank Holders of Tamil Nadu State Government Universities.

Statistical Tools: The collected data were analyzed by applying the following simple statistical tools.

- **Simple Percentage Analysis:** To assess the attitude of the Top Scorers towards societal cancer.
- **Sign Test:** To test the significant difference in the attitude of the Top Scorers towards societal cancer.

R. Malini
R. Raghadevi

The 'Z' value is computed by using the following formula.

$$Z = \text{Number of '+' sign} - \mu / \sigma$$

$$\mu = 0.5n; \ \sigma = \sqrt{0.25n}$$

Limitations of the study

- The study did not cover the student community as a whole it covers only the top scorers.
- The top scorers belongs to the realm of post-graduation commerce are selected as sample respondents.
- The private and deemed universities are excluded from this study.
- Search Fee is also a limitation for collection of data.

3. Results and discussion

Top scorers' attitude towards societal cancer

Crimes like terrorism, corruption, child marriage, child labor, child and women harassment, drugs and alcohol, hunger and poverty, unhealthy food habits, unemployment and underemployment, deforestation, water wastage and poor sanitation, destruction of scarce natural resources and religious conflicts cause societal cancer. This societal cancer has the power to change the destiny of the nation in a negative manner especially for a developing country like India. But the education has the power to change the destiny of the nation in a positive way by enhancing human stratum. In this context, it is crucial to assess the attitude of the top scorers against the societal cancer and it is given in the Table 1.

Table 1. Attitude of the Top Scorers towards Societal Cancer – Percentage Analysis

Attitude towards Societal Cancer	Yes	No Opinion	No	Total
Against Terrorism	275 (90.16)	30 (9.84)	0 (0.00)	305 (100.00)
Against Corruption	219 (71.80)	67 (21.97)	19 (6.23)	305 (100.00)
Against Child Marriage	288 (94.43)	11 (3.61)	6 (1.97)	305 (100.00)
Against Child Labor	275 (90.16)	20 (6.56)	10 (3.29)	305 (100.00)
Against Child and Women Harassment	290 (95.08)	15 (4.92)	0 (0.00)	305 (100.00)
Against Drugs and Alcohol	183 (60.00)	25 (8.20)	97 (31.80)	305 (100.00)
Against Hunger and Poverty	292 (95.74)	10 (3.28)	3 (0.98)	305 (100.00)
Against Unhealthy Food Habits	185 (60.66)	83 (27.21)	37 (12.13)	305 (100.00)
Against Unemployment and Underemployment	155 (50.82)	148 (48.52)	2 (0.66)	305 (100.00)
Against Deforestation	268 (87.87)	32 (10.49)	5 (1.64)	305 (100.00)
Against Water Wastage and Poor Sanitation	292 (95.74)	13 (4.26)	0 (0.00)	305 (100.00)
Against Destruction of Scarce Natural Resources	223 (73.11)	69 (22.62)	13 (4.26)	305 (100.00)
Against Religious Conflicts	184 (60.33)	100 (32.79)	21 (6.88)	305 (100.00)

Source: Primary Data
(Figures in Parentheses are Percentages)

It is clear from the Table 1 that the percentage of 'Yes' response ranges between 50.82 and 95.74. The percentage of 'No' response ranges between 0.00 and 31.80. The percentage of 'No opinion' ranges from 3.28 to 48.52. It indicates that the opinion of top scorers towards societal cancer varies from one top scorer to another top scorer. The analysis reveals that most of the top scorers are against societal cancer.

The percentage analysis disclosed that majority of the top scorers expressed their opinion against hunger and poverty (95.74 per cent) which is a positive sign to eradicate poverty and crimes to shape the society.

The percentage analysis exposed that 95.74 per cent respondents opined against water wastage and poor sanitation.

More than 90 per cent of the respondents had negative attitude against child / women harassment and child marriage. It indicates that they are ready to safeguard women and children.

The result further revealed that, none of the respondents are supporting terrorism, child and women harassment and water wastage and poor sanitation which are really an appreciable attitude of the educated community.

It is surprising to note that, less than 2% of the respondents had negative attitude towards unemployment and underemployment, hunger and poverty, deforestation and child marriage.

The most of the respondents neither expressed positive nor negative attitude against unemployment and underemployment problem (48.52 per cent), religious conflicts (32.79 per cent) and unhealthy food habits (27.21 per cent). The result indicated that the respondents are accustomed to live with this problem.

21.97 per cent respondents neither supported corruption nor against corruption. Some researchers argued that, corruption can have a positive effect by generating parallel and neutral economic flows. It provides opportunities to allow the private to point out the inefficiencies of Government and allow correcting its failures. The result of the present study indicated that the top scorers also having the same mentality which is supporting the above argument. But, corruption is not a healthy sign for the developing country like India.

London International Conferences, 28-30 January 2021, hosted online by UKEY Consulting and Publishing, London, United Kingdom

Finally, the shocking truth of the study is nearly 2/3rd of the respondents are not against drugs and alcohol and 12.13 per cent respondents are not against unhealthy food habits.

The attitude of the human stratum towards societal cancer may not be homogenous. The positive attitude towards societal cancer especially terrorism, corruption, hunger and poverty never be supported by any patriot. It induces the researchers to ascertain whether there is any significant difference in the attitude of the top scorers towards societal cancer and the result of the Sign test is given in the following Table.

Table 2. Attitude of the Top Scorers towards Societal Cancer – Sign Test

Attitude towards Societal Cancer	Number of '+' Signs	Number of '-' Signs	N	Z - Value	Result
Against Terrorism	275	0	275	16.59	Significant
Against Corruption	249	15	264	12.97	Significant
Against Child Marriage	288	6	294	16.45	Significant
Against Child Labor	275	10	285	15.70	Significant
Against Child and Women Harassment	290	0	290	17.04	Significant
Against Drugs and Alcohol	183	97	280	5.14	Significant
Against Hunger and Poverty	292	3	295	16.82	Significant
Against Unhealthy Food Habits	185	37	222	9.93	Significant
Against Unemployment and Underemployment	155	2	157	12.22	Significant

Against Deforestation	268	5	273	15.92	Significant
Against Water Wastage and Poor Sanitation	292	0	292	17.10	Significant
Against Destruction of Scarce Natural Resources	223	13	236	13.67	Significant
Against Religious Conflicts	184	21	205	11.38	Significant

Source: Primary Data

In order to test the above hypothesis, the sign test has been applied and the results are given in the Table 2. It displays that the Z-value is not within the accepted region of null hypothesis ($Z = -1.96$ to $Z = 1.96$) for all the statements. It indicates that there are significant differences in the attitude of the top scorers towards societal cancer. This is proved by the number of 'Yes' responses of the respondents to these statements. The result revealed the commitment of educated people over the society and nation. Hence, it is concluded that the top scorers are against societal cancer like terrorism, corruption, child marriage, child labor, drugs and alcohol, hunger and poverty, unhealthy food habits, child and women harassment, unemployment and underemployment, deforestation, water wastage and poor sanitation, religious conflicts and destruction of natural resources.

4. Suggestions

The suggestions given on the basis of analysis of the top scorers' attitude against drugs and alcohol, unhealthy food habits, unemployment and destruction of natural resources is highlighted here,

- Educated community should not consume drugs and alcohol. They should practice yoga, meditation on regular basis.
- Educated should eat organic food and concentrate on nutritious and balanced diet.
- Educated people should become job providers in lieu of job seekers to build better nation.
- Educated people should buying recyclable products, supporting environment friendly businesses and committed to safeguard the natural resources.

5. Conclusion

The percentage analysis revealed that 95 percent of the respondents had negative attitude towards hunger, poverty, child/women harassment, water wastage and poor sanitation. But, 30 percent of the respondents' unfavorable attitude towards corruption, destruction of natural resources and unhealthy food habits reduce the feasibility of attaining the sustainable development in the society. The result is supported by the 'Z' value of Sign test. Therefore, educated people should take part in politics and unite together utmost against societal cancer. Besides, they should fine tune themselves against societal cancer to attain societal wellbeing for the sustainable development.

References

Lander L, Howsare J, Byrne M. (2013). The impact of substance use disorders on families and children: from theory to practice. Soc. Work Public Health. 28(3-4): 194-205. doi:10.1080/19371918.2013.759005

World Health Organization, Draft Resolution on Further promotion of equalization of opportunities by, for and with persons with disabilities and mainstreaming disability in the development agenda

www.emerald.com/insight/content/doi/10.1108/IJSE-04-2017-0167/full/html

www.euractiv.com/section/agriculture-food/news/bad-eating-generates-huge-costs-tosociety-experts-warn/

www.girlsnotbrides.org

www.ibac.vic.gov.au/preventing-corruption/corruption-hurts-everyone

www.mydailyalerts.com

www.nature.com/scitable/blog/our-science/no_trees_no_humans/

www.ourworldindata.org/drug-use

www.rm.coe.int/education-against-corruption-en/168078299e

www.verywellmind.com/impact-on-society-63268#citation-7

London International Conferences, 28-30 January 2021, hosted online by UKEY Consulting and Publishing, London, United Kingdom

London International Conferences

londonic.uk

ukeyconsultingpublishing.co.uk

IFS (Integrated Farming System): Utilization of by-Products and Wastes to Attain Self-Sustainability

R. A. Aruna

Agriculture College and Research Institute,
Vazhavachanur, Tiruvannamalai
raaruna2000@gmail.com

Abstract

Industrialization of agriculture during the Green Revolution increased the production but it has created problems like pollution and climate change. So, for the future we need a resilient and sustainable food system. We can achieve that by working along with nature and not against it. There will not be any waste in any natural ecosystem. Waste is a concept that belongs only to artificial ecosystems. In IFS, the waste of one enterprise becomes the input of another enterprise, making it a self-sustainable farming system.

Keywords: agriculture, waste, self-sustainability

London International Conferences, 28-30 January 2021, hosted online by UKEY Consulting and Publishing, London, United Kingdom

1. Introduction

Population is ever increasing, but land is limited. So, there is no scope for horizontal expansion of land for agriculture. Moreover, Industrialization of agriculture has created problems like pollution and climate change. Self-sufficiency and sustainability are now gaining importance more than ever. Self-sustained development is the goal of many countries. Utilizing wastes is an important strategy to attain that. So, there is a need for a farming system that is self-sustainable. Integrated Farming System can be the solution.

2. Need for IFS

Many farmers plant only one crop in the same place year after year. Planting the same crop in the same place each year sucks nutrients from the earth and leaves soil weak and unable to support healthy plant growth, which in turn forces farmers to use chemical fertilizers to encourage plant growth and yield. These fertilizers, in turn, disrupt the natural makeup of the soil and contribute further to pollution. Monocropping also creates the spread of pests and diseases, which must be treated with yet more chemicals. The effects of monocropping on the environment are severe when pesticides and fertilizers make their way into ground water or become airborne.

3. Utilizing wastes

In IFS, the waste of one enterprise becomes the input of another for making better use of resources. Waste material/by products of crops and animals are recycled and used as inputs for other components of integrated farming system. So, this will help overcome the problems of small resource poor farmers, development of a more holistic, and interacting approach.

London International Conferences, 28-30 January 2021, hosted online by UKEY Consulting and Publishing, London, United Kingdom

3.1. Crop component

Crops that suit the given agro-climatic conditions and the socioeconomic status of the farmer can be grown and the by-products can be used as inputs in other enterprises, sometimes in the same enterprise too.

3.1.1. Multi-layer farming

Multi-layer farming can be a way of recycling the wastes within the crop component itself. Multi-layer farming is also called multi-storied cropping and multi-tire farming. Growing plants of different height in the same field at the same time is termed as Multi-layer cropping. It is one type of intercropping. It is generally practiced in orchards and plantation crops for maximum use of solar energy even under high planting density.

This Multi-layer cropping technique allows the farmers to get a good result of harvest and more earning on the same piece of land by making optimum available sources. Multi-tier cropping has been mentioned in Kutrala Kuravanji, a form of Tamil poetry written with Kutralanathar as the Hero. Kutralanathar is Lord Shiva present in the temple at Kutralam.

Module 1

We visited Purvabhumi, the 'adisil vanam' (edible food forest), which spread across 107 acres at Mudukulam village of Gandarvakottai taluk in Pudukottai district of Tamil Nadu, during our Study tour.

"I foresaw a problem for Agri business in the weather pattern, which paved the way to work with nature. After consulting experts, I tried different schools of scientific methods. The results were good but failed on economics. I realised that the only way out was ecological farming," recalls Mr. Senthilnathan, an entrepreneur, who now manages the farm.

By stopping the use of fertilisers and bringing down the labour cost by focusing on essentials, the cost of production came down. Every rupee that was spent afterwards was only towards planting seedlings, which is an investment rather than expenditure.

Simulating the features of a natural eco-system is the key. The farm has a variety of timber, fruits, vegetables, spices, sugarcane, coffee and cocoa.

A zero-cost principle adopted in the farm meant that coconuts would be collected after they fall from the tree and not plucked. A solar dryer is used to convert coconut into copra and oil is extracted. "Everything, except the oil, goes back to the soil. Ultimately, I want only profit, not revenue," says Mr. Senthilnathan. it adopts multi-tier cropping to enhance the soil quality and profit. "We do not allow sunlight to fall on the ground. The trees and plants harvest sunlight, converting energy into money," says Ammapettai Venkatachalam, an expert in organic farming.

More details about the food forest can be had from Purvabhumi, Mudukulam, Gandarvakottai Taluk, Pudukottai District 622203. Phone: 94425 70075 (P. Sunderraj, Farm Manager). Credits: The Hindu

3.1.2. Utilizing crop wastes

A crop by-product is derived along with the production or harvesting of a main crop.

Crop by-products can be used as feed, as litter, as a base for mushroom cultivation, as manure (incorporate /compost /pelleting), mulching, etc. While using it as a manure, Incorporation of crop waste as mulch is one way. Second way is going for composting. Compost can be done near the farm and can be used as manure. Large farmers can go for pelleting of organic wastes.

3.2. Animal component

India has a huge population of cattle. As a tradition every household possesses 1–2 cows/buffaloes or 3–4 goats. We get Milk, Curd, Ghee, Panchagavya Mix, Distilled Cow urine and cow dung. Dung of these animals are generally used as fuel by making dung cakes.

If these materials are recycled within the farm a sizable amount of money spent on chemical fertilizers can be saved.

When this cow dung is used to make bio gas it can be used as a fuel. Also, we will get bio digested slurry as a by-product in this process, which is an excellent organic manure and soil conditioner.

3.3. Integrated fish cum poultry farming

Apart from eggs and chicken, poultry also yields manure, which is a high fertilizer value manure in aquaculture. The poultry droppings from the poultry farms can be collected, stored in suitable places and is applied in the ponds at regular instalments. The other way is constructing the poultry housing structure partially covering the fish tank and directly recycling the dropping for fish culture, which will create a synergistic effect.

3.4. Fish-pig farming

Housing units of pigs can be constructed on the pond embankment in such a way that the wastes are directly drained into the pond. Pig dung acts as excellent pond fertilizer and raises the biological productivity of the pond and consequently increases fish production. Pond water is used for cleaning the pigsties and for bathing the pigs.

3.5. Sericulture

Pond mud or humus is the main nutrient source for mulberry cultivation. After fish harvest in winter each year, the pond mud is removed to form the "base soil" (base manure) of mulberry plants.

Silkworm excreta is used as feed for fish. Pond mud or humus is the main nutrient source for mulberry cultivation. After fish harvest in winter each year, the pond mud is removed to form the "base soil" (base manure) of mulberry plants.

4. Result

By mimicking the natural ecosystem, we can create a sustainable farming system in which each and every component will interact with one another in a synergistic way and wastes are being fed back as input. By doing so, we can get increased profit apart from nourishing the nature. As, profit= revenue - cost, reducing the costs by using wastes and by-products as inputs, will increase the profit.

London International Conferences, 28-30 January 2021, hosted online by UKEY Consulting and Publishing, London, United Kingdom

References

www.agritech.tnau.ac.in

http://www.imotforum.com/

Rangappa Yaraddi (2019) *The Impact of Integrated Farming System on Farmer's Agricultural Income*

www.thehindu.com

Thirikooda Rasappa Kavirayar *Thiru Kutrala Kuravanji*

The Characteristics of Parental Attitudes of Religious Families in Child-Rising (Muslim & Christian Families)

Serife METIN
Researcher- Kyrgyzystan
sbmetin2016@gmail.com

Yakup DOGANAY
Researcher- Kyrgyzystan

Abstract

Child-rising and enabling them to gain the required qualities and values have been one of the most important issues of families and societies throughout the history. Numerous researches have been done and much has been said in this field. It is quite normal that parents want their children to be like them, transmit the moralities and required personal characteristics from generation to generation. It is also known that there are a lot of factors effecting child-rising processes. Thus, in this study we investigate the effective factors such as religious level, economic situation, education level and cultural level, which we think influencing the parental attitudes. There is a perception that religious families can rise their children more successfully with more moral values and demanded personal characteristics. We have investigated this perception as well. How parental attitudes effect child-rising and their personal development have already been researched. First of all, we have implemented families religious level scales developed two pioneer scientists in this area to understand the religious level of the families. Then we have tried to understand the correlation between parental attitudes such as,

London International Conferences, 28-30 January 2021, hosted online by UKEY Consulting and Publishing, London, United Kingdom

democratic, authoritarian, conservative and tolerant and their religious score, economic, cultural and education level and status. We have given a survey and a questionnaire to 286 mothers and 107 fathers totally 393 parents having the children between 13-15 ages to find responds to our research questions and issues assuming they all have answered the questions with open hearts and honestly. The findings show that religious families generally develop authoritarian parental attitudes and their children pretend as if they obey their parents, but they do not develop positive demanded characters when they are independent and free in opposition to their parents' demands and our perceptions both in muslim and christian families. As a result, we can suppose that there is less correlation between religious levels of the families and child-rising more successfully. We can also say that families of all features; religious score, economic conditions, cultural and educational level need special pedagogical courses, coaching or some consultations for rising child more successfully, having better personal characteristics.

Keywords: Parental attitudes, child-rising, religious families, effective factors in child-rising.

London International Conferences, 28-30 January 2021, hosted online by UKEY Consulting and Publishing, London, United Kingdom

London International Conferences

londonic.uk   ukeyconsultingpublishing.co.uk

Future Is Near More Than Ever with Its Challenges for The World Citizens: Education as a Key

İbrahim Kurt

Stichting Cosmicus/NL

Abstract

The rapid changings in the life affect everything including individual, family, relations, work and societies. The humankind as a big family can face unexpected and unpredictable set of challenges. Both national and international contexts are globally chaining and changing the big world family. World citizen has become a necessity, but not as a choice. The question is "how does the individual respond and find new solutions to those challenges both as a member of the society and a responsible and active person in this world?"

It can be said that the wealth of the nation is the readiness and the will to learn with their capacity. The citizen will have an understanding of the nation, developing knowledge, the government work with its institutions, rights and duties of the citizens with the responsibility, respect to society and the state

London International Conferences, 28-30 January 2021, hosted online by UKEY Consulting and Publishing, London, United Kingdom

including the development of national identity. So, knowledge, values and innovation will be more necessary and critical for the societies. From this perspective, education is one of the best instruments for trying to solve humanity's problems and make sure its future as a nation or a society.

The purpose of citizenship education is to teach young generation about the 'in this local area and at this time' and about participating expectable and proper attitudes and behaviors in the localities of various citizenship contexts. However, "at this century and in this World" citizens in their specific society are facing and challenging a highly mobile and changing situations. Therefore, the twenty first century competence demands a world citizenship for its uncertain and unpredictable future. It is more important today to educate citizens for the future becomes an essential issue.

Keywords: Education, values, future, citizenship, world citizen

London International Conferences, 28-30 January 2021, hosted online by UKEY Consulting and Publishing, London, United Kingdom

londonic.uk   ukeyconsultingpublishing.co.uk

Making Entrepreneurship Happen and Be Acquired Throughout Education

Mehmet Tas
Researcher- Kazakhstan
mehmet.tas@sdu.edu.kz

Yakup Doganay
Researcher-Kyrgyzstan

Vahap Odar
Researcher- Kazakhstan

Abstract

Almost all of the countries aim to develop merchandise and economy. It is known that economically developed countries are better in education, technology, richer, stronger and more developed in almost all spheres of life. At the theoretical and practical background of developed economies there lie businessmen, merchandisers taking initiations in the business life and making investments with courage and right initiations. Whether doing business, merchandising and entrepreneurship could be learned through education, by practice from the childhood in real sector or even inherited are under questions. All the governments in the world search for the ways of

London International Conferences, 28-30 January 2021, hosted online by UKEY Consulting and Publishing, London, United Kingdom

developing their economies and believe that education could be one of them. From this point of view the governments begin to place lessons about economy and entrepreneurship nor just in economy departments but even in pedagogy departments. In this issue there are two points one; the teachers' education who will teach these lessons and second; the bachelor students' education of economy and entrepreneurship in departments of faculty of education. Because all the graduates of these departments may not find job in their field or one day at least some of them may need to begin their business in the field of education or whatever.

In this study the formation of economy and entrepreneurship in the faculty of pedagogy is investigated. After having placed the lesson for economy and entrepreneurship our students at our university have not graduated yet. Thus, we cannot search their life stories, the percentages of graduates beginning and doing their own business, their success, and effects of these lessons on their achievement stories in the entrepreneurship. So, we have tried to find out how students are affected, how their ideas and thoughts are formed and changed after having these lessons. Determining some criteria and preparing some specific questions students have been given some questionnaires.

The collected data was analysed. The findings are shown in tables, graphs and charts. The results, mentioned in our research, done via questionnaires and conclusion, show that the students of the Pedagogy faculty do not have the dream and idea of beginning their business in one day mostly. After having had the lessons of entrepreneurship, they begin to think about it to some extent but not all of them. We think that we need some more researches in this area, collaboration and cooperation of practice and theory of the lessons more in the real sector throughout the education.

London International Conferences, 28-30 January 2021, hosted online by UKEY Consulting and Publishing, London, United Kingdom

Mehmet Tas
Yakup Doganay
Vahap Odar

Making Entrepreneurship Happen and Be
Acquired Throughout Education

Keywords: entrepreneurship in education, entrepreneurial competence of a teacher, initiation

London International Conferences, 28-30 January 2021, hosted online by UKEY Consulting and Publishing, London, United Kingdom